Civility at Work

Civility at Work

How People Treatment is a Critical Success Driver for Business

Lewena Bayer

With contributions by Christian Masotti

BEP

BUSINESS EXPERT PRESS

Leader in applied, concise business books

Civility at Work: How People Treatment is a Critical Success Driver for Business

Copyright © Lewena Bayer, 2021.

Cover design by Charlene Kronstedt

Interior design by Exeter Premedia Services Private Ltd., Chennai, India

First published in 2021 by
Business Expert Press, LLC
222 East 46th Street, New York, NY 10017
www.businessexpertpress.com

ISBN-13: 978-1-95334-980-4 (paperback)
ISBN-13: 978-1-95334-981-1 (e-book)

Business Expert Press Human Resource Management and Organizational Behavior Collection

Collection ISSN: 1946-5637 (print)
Collection ISSN: 1946-5645 (electronic)

First edition: 2021

10 9 8 7 6 5 4 3 2 1

This one is for you Denby. You are where I find my courage, you are my compass. I love you like crazy cake bunny, Mom.

Description

In case you were not aware, research focusing on both Canadian and U.S. companies shows that a whopping 98 percent of people polled have experienced uncivil behavior on the job. And, according to the fourth annual study on *Civility in America: A Nationwide Survey*, conducted by global public relations firm Weber Shandwick and public affairs firm Powell Tate in partnership with KRC Research, civility in America continues to erode. This year's study found that 70 percent of the Americans believe incivility has reached crisis proportions. Alarmingly, 81 percent of the Americans think that incivility is leading to an increase in violence at work. Notably, 80 percent of the people are dissatisfied with their jobs.

Increasingly, people are choosing employers who understand that civility is good business. In *Civility at Work*, Lew Bayer describes the business case for civility and explains how organizations can increase employee retention, performance, and overall revenue by creating a workplace culture of *human kindness and civility*.

Keywords

civility; retention; social intelligence; workplace culture; respectful workplace; civility at work

Contents

Introduction

Fact: People treatment is a critical success driver for business. How organizations treat their employees generally, and more specifically how the policies and procedures, incentives, and best practices that direct and dictate the overall experience of human beings at work can make or break organizational success.

In three-time international bestselling book, *The 30 percent Solution; How Civility at Work Increases Retention, Engagement and Profitability* (Motivational Press 2016), we introduced the concept of civility (brand new to many) to organizations and individuals all over the world. Forward-thinking companies are understanding that to thrive in the new world of work, it is critical to embed civility in their core values, policies, procedures, and best practices. In our field work, we have seen measurable success in many organizations across sectors and around the globe. Some examples of these success stories are shared in the assignments and notes from the field sections of this book.

One of the reasons the team at Civility Experts Inc. have had success in the field is because the Civility Experts Inc. approach to civility is to do a comprehensive assessment to identify which of the four core civility competencies are lacking in an organization and to identify which of the four cultural components that support a successful civility initiative are, or are not, present in the workplace. Then, the team customizes a strategic civility solution, and so you are aware, this solution does not always include civility training. In addition, a thorough postsolutions evaluation is completed to understand the measurable impacts of the workplace civility initiative to the employees, to the organization, to the bottom line, and also to the community.

This process is based on the path to civility formula, depicted in Figure I.1.

Others in the field are reporting positive progress as well. As one example, The Weber Shadwick 2019 Civility in America Poll found that while the majority of Americans still agree that incivility is a serious problem in society overall, over the past three years, 89 percent polled say

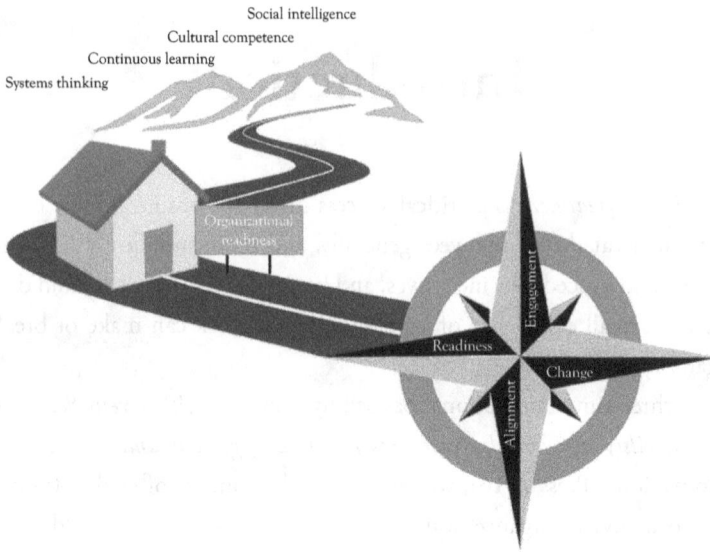

Systems thinking
Continuous learning
Cultural competence
Social intelligence

Organizational readiness

Readiness
Engagement
Change
Alignment

Figure I.1

their *workplace* is more civil. This is a significant change from 2015 where 87 percent of people polled said that their workplaces were uncivil.

The latest installment of the study also shows that respondents feel social media are contributing heavily to the cause of incivility, with 63 percent of the Americans reporting that the impact of social media on civility has been more negative than positive. Previous studies did not highlight media or social media as primary causes.

On the surface, that 89 percent of the people polled say their workplaces are more civil now than they were in 2015 seems like good news. However, at a closer look, the numbers just do not add up. I wonder if the perceived increase in civility has more to do with the general increase in discussions and provision of tools and policies related to civility resulting in a perception of increased civility, *or*, has civil behavior actually increased. Based on what the research is saying about increases in stress levels and mental wellness, I would suggest that things are not so different than they were 5 to 7 years ago, or that they are different, but not necessarily better.

With 2019 Weber Shadwick research stating that the average person encounters incivility an average of 2.4 times a day and 10.2 times during a work week, I propose that dealing with incivility has simply become a way of life for many. I would suggest that we will want to keep a close eye on the trends and expectations for civility online—this as our day-to-day work applications for online training, conference calls, chat, and so on has increased significantly.

In addition, the past decade has been fraught with significant social change. For example, events such as #metoo, the new *normal* in world politics, for example, presidential tweets, economic fluctuations, global pandemics, increasing world hunger, …and the list goes on, have significantly impacted the way we live, work, think, and interact. Specifically, many of us are barely surviving, and so, on the surface, social niceties seem a distant add-on.

One might think that with people interacting less due to being forced to work from home since the COVID-19 pandemic, things would be simpler. But, the reality is, working remotely carries with it all kinds of unexpected stressors, and sadly, with limited opportunities for real live interactions, remedy and repair can be problematic as well. As we move further into a work world where technology can simultaneously obligate or obscure transparency, where it is becoming increasingly difficult to differentiate between shades of truth and fabrication in everything from photos to profiles to documents and even integrity metrics, and where experiencing high touch, live human communication is quickly being replaced by replicas and automation, the remnants of positive people treatment are increasingly important.

Further, when there is low confidence related to job security and being able to pay the mortgage or put food on the table, people will often rationalize reduced expectations for social courtesy based on increased stress. This is not unreasonable, but regardless, most people still have to work for a living and having to encounter incivility face-to-face or online only serves to exacerbate already tenuous situations. As such, the workplace represents either a heaven or a hell with respect to our day-to-day experience. And, the reality—based on the research—is that for many people, work is not so heavenly.

What I know for sure, based on over 20 years in the field, is that:

- *Civility* in the workplace (whatever that workplace might look like) is an issue in workplaces all around the world.

As an aside, in case you did not know, Civility Experts Worldwide defines civility as:

○ A *conscious awareness* of the impact of one's thoughts, actions, words, and intentions on others; combined with;

○ A *continuous acknowledgment* of one's responsibility to ease the experience of others (for example, through restraint, kindness, nonjudgment, respect, and courtesy); and

○ A *consistent effort* to adopt and exhibit civil behavior as a non-negotiable point of one's character.

A civility initiative is a change imperative for companies that want to thrive in the new world of work.

- There is increasing evidence that skills once presumed to be *soft* or nice to have are in fact critical to long-term success.

- *Soft skills* can be described as a cluster of personal qualities related to willingness, attitude, personality, and social intelligence. Traditionally, civility has been listed as one of these *soft skills*.

- Research shows that the majority of one's financial success is because of skills in *human engineering*. Human engineering includes elements of your personality and your ability to communicate, negotiate, and lead. Human engineering is less reliant on technical knowledge—as previously understood, and more reliant on soft skills. Exhibiting civility represents human engineering—or what we at Civility Experts call positive people treatment.

- There is growing evidence that civility can have tremendous positive and measurable impacts on organizations, including:

  ○ Engagement, morale, workplace mental health, and retention

  ○ Revenue and profitability

  ○ Team orientation, problem-solving, and collaboration

  ○ Confidence, continuous learning, and competency

  ○ Respect, restraint, and responsibility

  ○ Psychological safety, stress management, and resilience

  ○ Change readiness and adaptive capacity

- *Companies that openly promote civil communication among employees earn 30 percent more revenue than competitors, are four times more likely to have highly engaged employees, and are 20 percent more likely to report reduced turnover[1].*

Civility at Work is intended to expand on the preceding issues detailed, to build on the core concepts and civility competencies outlined in *The 30 Percent Solution*, and to offer some new, current points for discussion. For example:

- In my work world, I see that people are experiencing genuine, unprompted civility less often than they did even five years ago. While we do see increases in respectful workplace policies and movements like #metoo, all kinds of calls for civility, including from the Pope, for people to disengage from their devices and connect with each other, as well as all kinds of brilliant and influential initiatives, including the Global Goodwill Ambassador program with tens of thousands of humanitarians joining forces, Global Citizen with the likes of George Clooney supporting, Kindness Communities, Character Education Partnerships, and Global Knowledge Exchange to mention a few, many people engage in civility on a surface level because it is the right thing to do—not because they have adopted civility as a core personal value. What does it say about human-kind that civility has become a marketing tool of sorts?
- In workplaces, we see many organizations adding aspects of *social impact* to their mission statements. We see businesses assigning in-house committees to run harassment or diversity campaigns. Organizations making donations to community causes, and so on. I am not saying that *all* of this is fraudulent or inauthentic, but sadly, much of it is. At the end of the day,

---

[1] Shandwick, Weber, and Tate, Powell. "Civility in America 2011," 2011. http://www.webershandwick.com/uploads/news/files/Civility_in_America_2011.pdf

the research shows that 80 percent of employees are unhappy at work. Clearly, outward efforts to convey intention to build better workplaces, to act morally and ethically, are not sufficient to change workplace culture and improve employee experience.

- Dr. Dhanapal Natarajan worries projected statistics about workplace wellness—specifically depression, will become a deadly reality. Natarajan, a board member of the Canadian Psychiatric Association, refers to the World Health Organization's prediction that by 2020, depression will become the second leading cause of disease worldwide. "In developing countries like Canada, it will be the leading cause," said the Regina, Saskatchewan, psychiatrist. One in five people have a diagnosable mental illness[2]. As such, depression tops the list of health-related productivity costs in the workplace. That was the finding in a medical study shortly after the economy tanked in the 2008 recession, and it is no different now. The annual cost of depression is estimated at 44 billion U.S. dollars in lost productivity to American companies according to the *National Institute of Mental Health*. The accelerated pace of work because of expanding technology can feed stress and anxiety in the workplace, but depression is a different animal. It is a clinical diagnosis "with specific criteria, which severely impact a person's ability to function." It can thwart an employees' ability to concentrate, be effective, and stay healthy enough to hold down a job[3]. If this depression can

---

[2] Cowan, Pamela. 2010. "Depression Will Be the Second Leading Cause of Disease by 2020: WHO." www.calgaryherald.com. July 10, 2010. http://calgary herald.com/health/Depression will second leading cause disease 2020/3640325/story.html.

[3] Martin, Judy. 2012. "Tackling Depression at Work as a Productivity Strategy." *Forbes Magazine*. October 24, 2012. https://forbes.com/sites/work-in-progress/2012/10/23/tackling-depression-at-work-as-a-productivity-strategy/#4e7d1b082294

be largely attributed to stress at work, and the cause of stress is incivility, why are employers not working harder to foster civility at work?

What Is the Book About?

Increasingly, individuals, organizations, and even governments recognize and agree with the business case for civility, including measurable gains in profitability and positive social impacts. And yet, aside from embracing the concept in a *show-and-tell* fashion, many still do not fully engage in teaching or requiring civility at work. In addition, research shows that work is the primary cause of stress for many working adults. Whether it is ill-prepared co-workers, office bullies, overt discrimination, rude customers, or any other of a multitude of workplace incivility occurrences, employers, and business owners have the ability (and some would argue the accountability) to create workplace cultures that foster civility and enable people to put their best foot forward at work—*Civility at Work* offers an essential toolkit of strategies, tools, insights, and information for small business owners, entrepreneurs, and managers who want to build a business based on character, civility, and common courtesies. It is never too late for embedding civility in processes and systems; however, incorporating ethics, social justice, equity, and fair play into your mission, values, and vision from the beginning can save a lot of time and set you up for success.

Civility at Work provides essential information, facts, stories, insights from the field, and practical tips related to the business of civility.

After reading this book, you can immediately start building a culture of civility in your workplace by incorporating some or all of the tools provided in the book, including:

- Strategies for embedding civility in your business plan, mission, values, and workplace communication plan
- Applying insights from the leading civility experts to your current workplace
- Identifying and adopting a practical definition of civility

- Assessing the extent to which incivility is impacting your bottom line
- Understanding trends and other influences that are impacting how we work
- Understanding how civility is a measurable competency

Who Is the Audience for This Book?

The book represents a ready-to-use tool kit with practical applications for:

- Business consultants
- Entrepreneurs
- Performance and productivity analysts
- Workplace trainers
- Social and communication training facilitators
- Customer service experts
- Business owners, managers, supervisors, and individuals who want to build a better workplace or build a successful business

Book Snapshot

Chapter Topic	Content Covered
Introduction	Rationale for *Civility at Workbook*
	Overview of book Contents
	Chapter summary chart
1. Time for Change	- Evidence that Incivility is Rampant
	- Elements of a Successful Civility Initiative
	- Civility in the Workplace is About Change
	- Readiness as an Indicator of Success for Civility Initiatives
	- The Civility Initiative Process at a Glance
	- Good news
1. 2. Defining Civility	- Outcomes of Civility Training
	- Dictionary Definitions of Civility
	- Civility Experts Worldwide Definition of Civility
	- The Difference Between Civility, Courtesy, Etiquette and Manners
	- How Does Civility Relate to Values?
	- Isn't Civility the Same Thing as Character?
	- How is Being Civil Different from Showing Respect?
	- The Difference Between Civility and Ethics
	- Civility and Emotional Intelligence
	- Civility and Positive Psychology
	- Civility and Being Nice
1. The Business Case	- Introducing Value of Civility Training to the Boss
	- Strategies for Persuading Others that Civility is Important
	- Assertions Made in Presenting Evidence that Civility Training Works
	- What are Soft Skills?
	- Han's List of Soft Skills
	- What the Research Shows About Soft Skills Relative to Technical Skills
	- Soft skills are Essential Skills
	- Civility requires Essential Skills
	- What will Successful Training Look Like?
	- Three Parts to Devising an Evaluation Plan
	- Impact of Essential Skills Training
	- The Business Case-Impact of Civility Training
1. Civility as a Change Initiative	- What does Change have to do with Civility?
	- The Stress of Change can be Positive.
	- Change = Learning
	- The New World of Work
	- Trends Impacting the way we Work
	- The Myth of Change
1. The Civility Culture Compass	- What Comes First, Uncivil Attitude, or Uncivil Behavior?
	- About Attitude
	- Why are People Rude at Work?
	- What is Organizational Culture?
	- Skills versus Competencies-what's the difference?
	- Using the Civility Culture Compass®
	- Four Conditions on the Compass

Figure I.2

Chapter Topic	Content Covered
1. The Civility Competency Matrix	- Four Key Skills Areas for Competency in Civility - Patterns of Impact-Civility Training at Work
1. About Continuous Learning	- What is Continuous Learning? - Why is Continuous Learning Important? - Relationship between Continuous Learning and Civility
1. About Social Intelligence	- What is Social Intelligence? - Why is Social Intelligence Important? - Relationship between Social Intelligence and Civility?
1. About Systems Thinking	- What is Systems Thinking? - Why is Systems Thinking Important? - Relationship between Systems Thinking and Civility
1. About Cultural Competence	- What is Cultural Competence? - Why is Cultural Competence Important? - Relationship between Cultural Competence and Civility
1. Assignments and Exercises	
1. Answer Keys and Tools You Can Use	

Figure I.2   **(Continued)**

Each chapter includes:

1. Notes from the field sections in each chapter; these highlight success stories related to civility in various workplaces.
2. A short quiz to test your knowledge.
3. Recommended Homework.
4. There are optional assignments in Chapter 10.

CHAPTER 1

Time for Change

Evidence That Incivility Is Rampant

One need only turn on the evening news to see that, as humankind, we are in crisis. All around the globe, this crisis is evident in increasing violence, racism, disregard for resources, workplace harassment, corruption, and inconceivable incivility in public discourse. In addition, and more alarming to me, we are also experiencing increasing incidences in widespread apathy, a lack of collective conscience, a deliberate turning away from our responsibilities to each other as human beings, and a troubling inability to engage effectively and civilly.

Related to this, and as an extreme example of incivility, my heart hurts knowing that an estimated 35,000 people die every day due to *genocides* in places like Myanmar and South Sudan. Of course, most of us are insulated from this type of extreme incivility, but incivility occurs on a continuum, and although not as extreme as war, we do feel its impacts closer to home too.

Looking at workplaces, which is the focus of this book, the civility crisis is evident, in that a whopping 80 percent of people are dissatisfied with their jobs[1]. Notably, the number one reason for this dissatisfaction is employees' perceived lack of respect and fair treatment. Because the research suggests most of us spend one-third of our lives at work (an average of 90,000 hours over a lifetime[2]), I would suggest that workplace incivility is a gateway to incivility in the community, to the public square,

---

[1] Premack, R. 2018. "17 Seriously Disturbing Facts about Your Job." *Business Insider. Business Insider.* August 2, 2018. http://businessinsider.com/disturbing-facts-about-your-job-2011-2?op=1#ixzz3XCZH6nbq

[2] "One Third of Your Life Is Spent at Work." n.d. Gettysburg College. https://gettysburg.edu/news/stories?id=79db7b34-630c-4f49-ad32-4ab9ea48e72b&pageTitle=1percent2F3 of your life is spent at work

to our schools, and so on. I would also suggest that this is true of work-places all around the world.

We carry the impacts of incivility with us wherever we go, and so, the toxicity created by incivility manifests as road rage, stress-related illness, social aggression, social isolation, inappropriate behavior in public places and on social media, bullying, harassment, racism… and the list goes on. We are also seeing the impacts of incivility in our daily interactions, and as you would guess, the research shows incivility is a contributing factor to everything from school shootings to measurable declines in community social capital, and to leadership trust indicators. Quite a gloomy picture overall.

Christine Porath, leading researcher in human performance and author of *Workplace Civility*[3], states,

> . . . more than two-thirds of people will cut back work effort, 80 percent of people lose time worrying about what happened, and 12 percent of people will report that they've left their job because of an uncivil incident… not only does incivility decrease perfor-mance, but people aren't nearly as innovative, even if they just wit-ness incivility. In team settings, it causes people to shut down, such that they don't share information or speak up as much. They don't discuss errors or inform each other of potential problems.

And then, the other issue is that even witnesses, as well as people who experience it, are far less helpful. They are actually three times less likely to help someone else, and their willingness to share drops by more than 50 percent. So, incivility pulls people off track, even for those people who are trying to push forward.

Research by Weber Shadwick and Powell Tate, in partnership with KRC Research, detailed in the 2019 Civility in America report[4], found that:

- The majority of Americans perceive incivility to be a problem in our society.

---

[3] "The Future of Work Is Human." 2019. *Workhuman*. September 3, 2019. https://workhuman.com/resources/research-reports/the-future-of-work-is-human

[4] "Civility in America 2019: Solutions for Tomorrow." 2019. *Weber Shandwick*. https://webershandwick.com/news/civility-in-america-2019-solutions-for-tomorrow/

- The frequency of uncivil encounters per week rose sharply in 2018 and remains at this level, with 10.2 average weekly encounters. Notably, the location of uncivil interactions has shifted over the years. Uncivil online interactions have increased from an average of 4.4 weekly interactions in 2013 to a high of 5.5 in 2019.
- More than one half of the Americans (54 percent) expect civility to get worse[5].
- Listed next were the top 10 consequences of incivility—according to respondents:
  - Online bullying/cyberbullying
  - Harassment (verbal, physical, or sexual)
  - Violent behavior
  - Hate crimes
  - Intimidation and threats
  - Intolerance
  - People feeling less safe in public places
  - Discrimination and unfair treatment of certain groups of people
  - Less community engagement
  - Feelings of isolation and loneliness

The preceding research cited is American based, but we see similar statistics around the world. For example:

Incivility results from kindcanada.org showed:

- Two-third employees report a decline in performance as a result of unkind workplaces.
- 48 percent of the employees who were exposed to an unkind co-worker were significantly more likely to decrease their work efforts.
- 38 percent of the employees noted that they intentionally decreased the quality of their work.

---

[5] Ibid.

A study of British workers found that 40 percent had experienced incivility or disrespect over a two-year period, with such behavior particularly common in the public sector[6].

In a study of Australian workers, researchers from Edith Cowan University found that 70 percent had experienced rudeness or mistreatment by their coworkers[7].

A Canadian study by Bar-David Consulting and *Canadian HR Reporter* shows incivility affects key business indicators as reported by human resource professionals:

90 percent say it hurts collaboration.

78 percent say it affects talent retention.

52 percent say it affects brand reputation.

92 percent agree incivility has negative effects on productivity.

80 percent report an impact on absenteeism[8].

Data collected from employees from various organizations in Singapore shows that incivility is not a rare phenomenon in Asian cultures[9].

The results of study of Korean workplaces offered evidence of a positive relationship between the experience of workplace incivility and the intention to leave the organization. More specifically, it was found that if one experiences workplace incivility, then he or she is more likely to leave the organization[10].

---

[6] "The High Cost of Workplace Rudeness." 2014. BBC Worklife. BBC. April 1, 2014. http://bbc.com/capital/story/20140401-how-rude-why-polite-pays

[7] http://sciencewa.net.au/topics/social-science/item/2174-reactions-to-workplace-incivility-explored/2174-reactions-to-workplace-incivility-explored

[8] Bar-David, S. 2011. "Benefits Column: Abrasive Employees Hurt Productivity." *Benefits Canada Benefits Column Abrasive Employees Hurt Productivity Comments.* http://benefitscanada.com/benefits/health-wellness/benefits-column-the-impact-of-workplace-incivility-62273

[9] Lim, S,, and A. Lee. 2011. "Work and Nonwork Outcomes of Workplace Incivility: Does Family Support Help?" *Journal of Occupational Health Psychology.* U.S. National Library of Medicine. January 2011. http://ncbi.nlm.nih.gov/pubmed/21280947

[10] Shim, J., and H.J. Chang. n.d. "The Relationship Between Workplace Incivility and the Intention to Leave; Implication to HRD." ICERI2011 Proceedings. IATED. http://library.iated.org/view/SHIM2011REL

If the statistics outlined in this chapter are any indication, WORK seems to be at the root of the problem. The majority of us are physically exhausted, stressed, and overextended. And, many of us are miserable in our jobs. We are worn down and less resilient than we once were. We are burnt out. Our health is at stake, our home lives are suffering. We do not have the time or energy to take care of ourselves, and so, the idea that we would extend courtesies or consideration to take care of others seems a cost many of us simply cannot bear.

To meet the demands of our fast-paced, demanding, and every-changing work lives, we have resorted to bad habits. I describe these habits as the "coping selfies"; self-preservation, self-righteousness, self-promotion, self-centeredness, self-pity, self-denial, self-destruction, and so on. These selfies represent many of the "social survival" behaviors desperate people engage in. These habits result in individuals addressing their self-interests at the expense of others. Overall, we are exercising significantly less respect, less restraint, and less responsibility. These are the three tenants that underpin civility—this according to Dr. Pier Forni, Professor at Johns Hopkins, and author of Choose Civility. Over the past 20 years' training, researching, and speaking on civility in the workplace, I am convinced that the conditions and cultures of our workplaces are causing much of the desperation the mass of men and women are experiencing these days.

Notably, 80 percent of the people are dissatisfied with their jobs[11].

About 25 percent of the employees say work is their main source of stress, and 40 percent say their job is *very or extremely stressful*[12]. This stress impacts our health; for example, in the United Kingdom, over

---

[11] Premack, R. 2018. "17 Seriously Disturbing Facts about Your Job." *Business Insider*. Business Insider. August 2, 2018. http://www.businessinsider.com/disturbing-facts-about-your-job-2011-2?op=1#ixzz3XCZH6nbq

[12] "Quality of Working Life." 2014. *Encyclopedia of Quality of Life and Well-Being Research*, 5320–20. https://doi.org/10.1007/978-94-007-0753-5_103371

13 million working days are lost every year because of stress. Stress is believed to trigger 70 percent of the visits to doctors and 85 percent of serious illnesses[13].

Alarmingly:

- 40 percent of employees say their job is *very or extremely stressful*[14].
- Workplace stress is believed to trigger 70 percent of the visits to doctors and 85 percent of serious illnesses[15].
- The Center for Disease Control states that adult depression, largely attributed to stress at work—which in turn is largely attributed to incivility—will rank second only to ischemic heart disease as the leading cause of workplace disability in 2020. If this statistic in and of itself does not present a strong business case for civility at work, I do not know what does.

Is Rudeness Really an Issue? Assessment

Rude behavior can come in all shapes and sizes. While some people are fully aware that their behaviors offend, others are unaware that people consider their actions rude. How many of the following behaviors have you experienced in the past two weeks? Place a checkmark next to each behavior you have witnessed. If you have witnessed any more than once, write the number of the instances in the blank. Answer honestly—even if you have committed some of the rude behaviors.

What other behaviors have you experienced while at work?

In addition to the health impacts, incivility also contributes to low engagement in the workplace.

---

[13] "Work-Related Stress, Anxiety or Depression Statistics in ..." 2019. https://www.hse.gov.uk/statistics/causdis/stress.pdf

[14] "Quality of Working Life." 2014. *Encyclopedia of Quality of Life and Well-Being Research*, 5320–20. https://doi.org/10.1007/978-94-007-0753-5_103371

[15] "Work-Related Stress, Anxiety or Depression Statistics in ..." 2019. https://hse.gov.uk/statistics/causdis/stress.pdf

Table 1.1 *Is Rudeness Really an Issue*

✔	Rude Behavior	Occurrences
	Tardiness	
	Swearing	
	Inappropriate dress	
	Bad attitude	
	Lack of preparation	
	Interrupting someone as he or she speaks	
	Barging into someone's workspace	
	Someone ignoring someone else	
	Someone not listening	
	Disrespect for or destruction of the organization's property	
	Rude tone of voice	
	Gossip or talking about someone when he or she is not present	
	Yelling or other emotional outbursts	
	Someone wasting someone else's time	
	Lack of information sharing	
	Sharing of inappropriate personal stories (e.g., drug-related or sexual in nature)	
	Placing blame on someone else	
	Messes left in common areas	
	Failing to hear someone out; quickly shooting down others' ideas	

There are many indicators of low engagement. Sometimes, it is true that attendance and number of sick days or stress-leave requests seem like obvious signs that people are not engaged. But, these are not always accurate; for example, there may be legitimate physical or psychological reasons a person is not coming to work. Because we understand engagement to mean employees is actively choosing to contribute in a positive way beyond their basic job requirements, we (Civility Experts Inc. field team) find a stronger indicator of engagement is the overall level of trust. This is because high levels of trust typically correlate with employees stating that:

- ° They feel valued as individuals.
- ° They feel their contribution has value.
- ° They feel empowered.
- ° They feel that they are treated fairly.
- ° They feel they are compensated fairly.
- ° They feel empowered to self-direct and make decisions.
- ° They have a sense of shared purpose.
- ° They feel they can overcome workplace challenges.
- ° They feel supported.
- ° They are happy at work.

But, there is light. I believe, and I hope you will too, in the power of one. I believe that each of us has the power to be better, and to do better—for ourselves and for each other, and I—as I hope is also true for you, believe that most of us would do better if we knew better. *Company culture* includes a variety of elements, including:

- Work environment
- Company mission
- Values
- Ethics
- Expectations
- Goals
- (And, Masotti and Bayer would add "employee experience" as an aspect of workplace culture)

Generally, *the character or culture of an organization is what defines the overall day-to-day experience of the employees who live in that culture.* From a civility point of view, this experience results largely from *people-treatment* (described in the introduction). And, it is often the character (plus aspects of personality) of the individuals who lead an organization that influences the culture. Over time, because *like attracts like*, the majority of employees either have similar character as leadership *or* employees take on the qualities and values of those leading them, and as such, the organizational culture becomes a reflection of the character of the people living and leading in that workplace.

Traditionally, across sectors, management teams have focused on key performance indicators related to output, for example, how many parts are produced or how many injuries are incurred, how much market share is retained, and so on. However, many forward-thinking organizations are now a new approach to training that can address key performance indicators related to the people side of their businesses.

These indicators include:

- Engagement
- Innovation
- Collaboration
- Retention
- Morale
- Stress at work
- Health at work, for example, sick days
- Ability to manage change
- Learning
- Teamwork
- Autonomy
- Communication
- And, overall workplace culture

As such, these organizations frequently have good data, good methods or tools, and processes in place, but some (or all) of these are rendered less valuable due to poor management of *the people aspect of business.* The employees in an organization represent an invaluable resource, which when mishandled and underleveraged can lead to debilitating and long-lasting issues in a workplace.

Research shows that when organizations embed civility—including incorporating specific aspects of civility in an overall communication approach and protocols, and engaging in strategic skill building, the *people* aspect is readily addressed, and the result is measurable impact to social cohesion, employee involvement, trust, collaboration, retention, productivity, engagement, and profitability.

Elements of a Successful Civility Initiative

It must be understood and acknowledged that to take root, you cannot change workplace culture just be delivering civility competencies training. Training is one part of a comprehensive civility change initiative.

A civility change initiative must be strategic, well planned, and long term, and there has to be a clarified rationale for civility in the workplace. (This will make more sense after you define civility; more on this in Chapter 2.) Just like most change initiatives, incorporating civility into your workplace culture is going to take some time, money, and energy. You will likely have to delegate people and resources, and you will have to manage both the process and people sides of the change. To be successful, you will have to have a plan that includes identifying stakeholders, assigning roles, completing assessments, setting goals, implementing the plan, delivering alignment communications, planning and delivering training, and evaluating. How complex and costly each of those components are will depend on the context and on your business priorities. To be clear, when we talk about how complex a civility initiative might be, we are referring to how many components are included in the plan. This is different from the level of difficulty or how complicated the initiative might be. Civility as a change initiative might be complex, in that there are a lot of components to consider, but it is not necessarily complicated.

We must understand and acknowledge that the work will be ongoing and continuous. The reality is, due to the fact that the situation, the people, the priorities, and the conditions in a workplace are constantly changing, you are never really finished with civility as a change initiative. Let me repeat that, there is no end point. You are *never* really finished with civility as a change initiative. And, this is an extremely important realization. I believe that this realization is one of the biggest barriers most organizations face in moving forward with civility initiatives. Planning and implementation can be very hard work initially. It is going to cost some time and money, and you have to be wholly committed long term. This can be prohibitive for some. But, if you can get past this hurdle, and if use the Civility Culture Compass®—discussed in Chapter 5 as your guide—you will be successful. And, the rewards are often immutable, measurable, positive, and significant.

Civility in the workplace is about change. Okay. But, we deal with change all the time, so why is this a big deal?

The big deal is that 70 percent of the change initiatives fail. Somewhere along the way, the change management strategies and processes we have been using have become ineffective. And, 70 percent is a lot of failure. And, a lot of time, a lot of resources, a lot of frustration, and a lot of desperation. (You may recall from the introduction how problematic desperation can be.)

Where this failure applies to civility initiatives, I have come to understand that there are two main reasons organizational civility projects fail. This understanding could potentially be applied to other types of change initiatives, but for the moment, we are, of course, focusing on civility as a change initiative. The reasons are:

a. Change management processes, efforts regarding application of these processes, and for the most part, competencies required to apply the processes, are all rendered less effective, without commitment to the process, and more importantly, without understanding of both the desired outcome of the change and the value that outcome. Put simply, *engagement is essential to facilitating lasting, meaningful culture change.*

b. Many individuals, teams, and organizations simply do not have the capacity—in terms of their skill set to make the required change. *Skills-wise, the organization is not change-ready.*

c. Engagement is essential to facilitating lasting, meaningful change. Effective change happens when an organization and individuals in the organization are *ready* competency-wise, for change.

Let us first look at point (a). What is engagement? For our purposes, *engagement* means that individuals (employees) actively and consciously choose to contribute to the workplace in a meaningful way. In doing so, they show that they believe in the organization, they acknowledge that they, as individuals, have value and are valued, and they have an understanding of, and share, the organizational values and goals. So, engagement goes far beyond attendance. Showing up and doing just what you are required to do is not engagement. Our research has shown that there are definite causal factors when employees become disengaged, and the most powerful of these relate to:

a. How clearly the organizational goals have been communicated.
b. The extent to which employees recognize their value and feel valued.
c. Whether or not the day-to-day contributions of employees are properly aligned with the organizational goals—this creates a shared purpose.

These three factors contribute to the overall levels of trust and help create workplace culture. (More on this in Chapter 5.) When any or all of the aforementioned factors are not in place, we start to see disengagement and other symptoms of incivility begin to emerge.

Imagine a workplace where some or all of the symptoms of viral incivility are present.

Some common and measurable symptoms of incivility have been identified over 20 years of field work by Civility Experts Inc.

Civility Symptoms Survey

- Persistent miscommunication, such as nonresponsiveness, misunderstandings, arguments, and withholding of information
- Diminished morale and/or mood, for example, negative attitudes, lack of energy
- Poor engagement, lowered confidence, and low trust
- Measurable lack of accountability
- Decreased productivity
- Increased lateness and laziness
- Reduced quality and quantity of output
- Diminished collaborative effort
- Increased customer service complaints, for example, due to visible decrease in product and/or service standards
- Growing gap in alignment between personal and/or corporate goals and leadership's abilities
- Lack of integrity and ethics
- Inability to adapt effectively to change
- Inability to navigate cultural and communication barriers

- Increased difficulty recruiting and hiring competent personnel
- Difficulty identifying and practicing core values
- Lowered common sense
- Failure to attend to social cues and follow social conventions
- Increased disengagement, for example, as indicated by difficulty maintaining relationships, less involvement in social, civic, and community events

Over the years, we have learned that the more symptoms there are present, and the greater the frequency of observance of the symptoms, the more these symptoms support the statistics referenced in the introduction, which suggested that 80 percent of the people are dissatisfied with their work. Dissatisfied means that employees do not feel valued, they do not feel adequately compensated, they do not feel safe at work, they are experiencing unmanageable stress, they are being bullied, they do not feel secure, do not trust their boss, and so on. If employees are dissatisfied, it is unlikely that they are focused on skill-building and productivity. They are more likely focused on those desperate *coping selfies* we referenced earlier—the social survival behaviors; self-preservation, self-promotion, self-indulgence, self-absorption, self-pity, self-interest, and so on. Self-focus does not lend well to team orientation or collective goals.

An organization might implement respectful workplace or conflict management training in an effort to alleviate one of the incivility symptoms, and this training might even be deemed *good* because employees gain some knowledge or skill. But, employees may not be inclined to transfer that skill and knowledge to the workplace in a meaningful way because they are not sufficiently engaged. Most employers would agree that it does not matter how much people learn if they cannot connect and use their new knowledge and skills effectively on the job. Unfortunately, a lot of time and money are often spent on good but ineffective training before leadership realizes there has not been sufficient transfer of learning. Without transfer of learning, there likely will not be much measurable impact or benefit to the workplace. And, you need engagement to ensure meaningful transfer of learning.

When building a culture of civility in the workplace is the goal, much of the conflict management, general communication, and diversity training delivered in workplaces these days constitute good—but ineffective—solutions. If employees are not engaged, it does not matter how many conflict resolution strategies, how much cultural knowledge, or how many communication courses you offer them, you will likely not experience a significant decrease in incivility in your workplace.

Full engagement means employees are willing and wanting, not only to participate, but also to contribute through that participation in a way that is useful and valuable—beyond meeting the minimum requirements to stay employed. Activity does not equal engagement. Attendance is not necessarily an indication of engagement. Buy-in, trust, and active, conscious, meaningful contribution—these are indicators of engagement.

Readiness as an Indicator of Success for Civility Initiatives

That individuals, teams, and/or the organization overall are not *change-ready* skills-wise is the second reason we (the team at Civility Experts Worldwide) find that many civility initiatives fail. By *change readiness*, we are referring to competency in specific skills that underpin the ability to exhibit civility at work. We have identified four core competency areas necessary to change uncivil workplaces into positive, healthy, civil organizations. These four competence areas are social intelligence, cultural competence, systems thinking, and continuous learning. These are discussed in detail in Chapter 7, *The Civility Competency Matrix*.

The basic idea is that while we hope and expect that people who adopt civility as a core value will necessarily adopt a positive, proactive attitude, attitude change is not enough. We need behavior change too. We need everyone in the organization to be able to exhibit skills that reflect their civil attitude. Building competency in the four key skill areas outlined in the *Civility Matrix*® enables individuals, teams, and organizations to behave more consistently in ways that support a culture of civility in a workplace.

The Civility Initiative Process at a Glance

As you make your way through the next few chapters of this book, you will come to understand how to devise and implement a civility initiative in your workplace. If you are not yet clear on what civility is, Chapter 2,

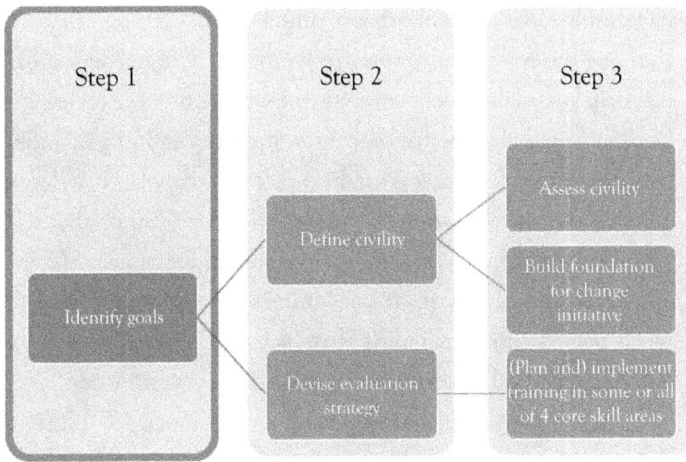

Figure 1.1

Defining Civility, should be helpful. And, if you are not yet sure about the benefits of starting a civility initiative, we present the business case in Chapter 3.

Please note Figure 1.1, which outlines a general three-step process for devising a civility initiative:

There are just three general steps in the civility initiative process, seems easy enough, right!

Step 1 in the process *is identifying your goals.* This means starting with the end in mind. In the case of devising a civility initiative, we know in advance that because of the nature of change in our workplaces, and because civility competencies are soft skills that are never fully developed, we are *always* going to identify some need related to one or more of four core skill areas. And, based on 18 years in the field combined with the research, we also know that training in the civility competency areas does result in specific outcomes, and these outcomes are most likely on your *end in mind* wish list.

To begin, ask yourself (or work with your team to answer) the following questions. If you do not have an answer for each, you are not ready to move on to Step 2:

1. *What exactly do you want to happen as a result of the initiative?* Stated differently, what is the purpose of building a culture of civil-ity? For example, reduced turnover, higher productivity, increased

engagement, more collaboration, and so forth. Sometimes, using a tool like the *Symptoms of Viral Incivility Checklist* referenced earlier can help you identify what you do not want. And/or, a review of the list of 32 possible positive outcomes of civility training included at the beginning of Chapter 2 can help you identify what you do want.

2. *Why do you want whatever it is that you want?* Think about how, and if, a successful civility initiative is something you should invest your time and money in. If your immediate response is something like: "Because it seems the right thing to do" or "We have a lot of bullying and legal issues and this seems like a necessary next step" or "We don't want to be the only company without one," please take some additional time to think about whether these motivators will be enough to propel you through the process. In the past, when organizations adopt civility as a means of running away from something as opposed to running toward something, we frequently do not get past the first two stages of the process.

3. *What specifically is the benefit or impact to the employee(s), and/or to the organization, if you get what you want?* For example, if you say you want more collaboration, why would this be good for employees? How does it benefit the organization? And, what if you get what you want? Will you actually do something with it? Will you be able to manage it? Will increasing collaboration, for example, potentially result in any unforeseen costs? Will it require employees work differently and can you support that? Is the management team on board?

4. *What evidence do you have that the outcome you want could, or would, in fact result from the initiative?* We want to be sure that we can clarify what exactly civility will look like in the workplace. This enables us to measure success. Consider doing a comprehensive situational analysis so that you can understand the current situation and recognize factors that could hinder or facilitate the impact of your civility training plan. (The Civility Culture Compass® can help you with this.)

5. *Are there any drawbacks or unfavorable consequences to you, the team, or the organization if you get what you want?* Are you prepared if the outcomes are different than you expected? As an example, what if employees start to work better as a team? What will you do with

the potential time savings? What if the teams are even 10 percent more productive? Positive change typically results in more positive change, and you have to be prepared to manage these changes ongoing. As an example, if people become more competent, do you have to pay bonuses? Will you have to secure more accounts to keep up with increased productivity? Will you end up laying off employees because production is more efficient? Be sure to consider the trends, changes, and other influences impacting the organization, and forecast any impacts that could influence change in your workplace over the next five years at minimum.

6. *Are your goals realistic, for example, SMARTER; specific, measurable, attainable, realistic, time-set, and/or timely, evaluated, and rewarding/ rewarded?* Do you have a goal that is clearly defined? This is going to drive the whole process, so it is important to take some time to devise this SMARTER goal.

Recommended Homework

There is some good news!

The good news is that awareness is growing about the benefits of civility at work, and they are ready for change. Nearly eight in 10 employees with coworkers (78 percent) report that civility at work provides tangible upsides. Four in 10 say civility at work improves their work morale and increases their loyalty to their employer (40 percent each) and nearly as many say it improves their quality of work (36 percent)[16].

People-Treatment Self-Assessment

By L. Bayer, Civility Experts Inc. All rights reserved.

Review the following listing of positive people treatment behavior, and consider how frequently, and how consistently you exhibit these behaviors, and if you do not exhibit them, why don't you?

---

[16] "Civility in America 2019: Solutions for Tomorrow." 2019. Weber Shandwick. https://webershandwick.com/news/civility-in-america-2019-solutions-for-tomorrow/

Table 1.2 People Treatment Assessment

• Posture, for example, I present myself (physically) as open-minded, ready to engage, and approachable.
• Time management, for example, I show that I understand time is a valuable resource, for example, do not waste my time or time of others, be on time.
• Expectations, for example, have clear expectations for oneself and for others.
• Treat people fairly, for example, equal opportunity, use same criteria to measure equally.
• Honesty, for example, be honest, tell the whole truth whenever possible.
• Tone, for example, I consider tonal elements when I interact verbally with others including: 　○ Pace 　○ Word choice 　○ Volume 　○ Timing 　○ Privacy or confidentiality 　○ Emotionality 　○ Impact 　○ Relationship, for example, accountability and familiarity 　○ Cultural nuances 　○ Risk, for example, perceptions related to gender 　○ Expectations of listener, for example, generational aspects 　○ Mode of communication, for example, face to face, phone, and so on
• Indication of bias, for example, Am I aware that I change my approach depending who I am interacting with?
• Common courtesy, for example, eye contact, handshake, proximity, smile, introductions, please, thank you, offering food or beverage, and others
• Care with word choice, for example, consider frame of reference
• Perspectives on role, rank, status, and contribution
• Communication approach, for example, formal versus informal, conversational versus legal, personal versus professional
• Willingness to adapt to individual need, for example, if someone needs supports due to physical or physiological barriers
• Perception of differences, for example, do I see differences as advantages or as barriers?
• Ability to show respect, for example, by interacting in a way that leaves the other person feeling valued (I understand that respect is not something people need to earn; we are all deserving of respect because we are human beings.)
• Ability to build rapport, for example, ease and flow of interaction
• Response in stressful or emotional settings, for example, do I stay calm? Do I help others be calm? Can I exercise restraint?

Table 1.2 (*Continued*)

• Ability to build trust and to be perceived as trustworthy
• Openness, for example, authenticity and vulnerability
• Ability to effectively interpret verbal, nonverbal, tonal, and contextual cues
• Situational awareness, for example, recognize factors that might impact people
• Ability to adapt social style appropriately
• Cultural competence, for example, recognize, adapt, and work with differences
• Emotional intelligence, for example, be aware of my own issues and hot buttons
• Ability to empathize and share perspective
• Ego, for example, attitude about one's own importance
• Humility, for example, ability to acknowledge gifts and contributions of others over focusing on one's own gifts, talents, and contributions
• Willingness to learn
• Patience, for example, to listen
• Willingness to apologize
• Curiosity, for example, interest in learning and asking questions
• Readiness to forgive, for example, accept apologies with grace
• Recognition of human condition, for example, acknowledge that I cannot always understand or know what another person is experiencing
• Generosity, for example, ability to give with no expectation of return
• Systems thinking, for example, ability to consider impact of actions and decisions
• Social acuity, for example, ability to assess and interpret interpersonal connections and cost, benefits, and consequences of same
• Values, for example, can I articulate my values if necessary, and do I live my values?
• Ability to acknowledge and celebrate achievements and contributions of others
• Positive attitude, for example, look for the best in people and in situations
• Responsibility, for example, take care of myself, do not blame others or expect other to manage me (my daily life or actions or activities)
• Accountability, for example, own my own tasks and decisions
• Service orientation, for example, do I show through my actions that I am *other-focused* and can put needs of others before my own needs and wants when appropriate or required?

Increasingly, people are choosing employers who understand that civility is good business. In the remaining chapters of *Civility at Work*, we discuss the definition of civility, the business case for civility, and we explain how entrepreneurs and business owners can increase employee

retention, performance, and overall revenue by building civility competencies and creating a workplace culture of *human kindness and civility.*

Test Yourself

1. How many people die in genocides, which are global incivilities,
   every day?
   a. 10,000
   b. 5,000
   c. 35,000
   d. Over 100,000

2. When writing SMARTER goals for civility initiatives, the "E" refers to:
   a. Eliminate
   b. Evaluate
   c. Encourage
   d. Elaborate

3. Workplace "culture" is described by Masotti and Bayer as:
   a. How people dress and act at work
   b. The power division or hierarchy of a workplace
   c. The day-to-day experience of living in a workplace
   d. The tone of a company, for example, how people feel

CHAPTER 2

Defining Civility

What Is Civility?

To be meaningful in a workplace context, civility must be defined in a way that is comprehensive enough to make people think differently. And, at the same time, it must have immediate personal relevance for people, given whatever environment or situation they happen to be in. When a person hears the word, he or she needs to see the possibilities and imagine some of the outcomes of civility training (see the following list). The definition has to include elements that expand it from a vague, subjective notion of "niceness" to a practical, measurable concept with applications for skill development in a range of different contexts.

Dictionary Definitions of Civility

Oxford Dictionary Online: Civility—Formal politeness and courtesy in behavior or speech

Merriam Webster Online: Civility—Polite, reasonable, and respectful behavior

Dictionary.com: Civility—Courtesy; politeness

Cambridge Dictionary Online: Civility—the quality of being polite

None of these definitions captures the attitudinal and values components that are so important to the practical applications of civility. From a workplace training point of view, when civility is reduced to politeness, it is often categorized along with other social courtesies such as thank you notes, hygiene, eye contact, and handshakes—and in many organizational contexts, these are considered *nice to have*. Even if politeness is understood to be an important element of customer service, or maybe courtesy is recognized as one aspect of working well with others, it is still not usually deemed important enough as a standalone skill to warrant spending time, money, and energy on it.

This dismissal can have *big* consequences. In spite of the growing evidence that civility in the workplace can be a game-changer, if you are a training professional, a human resources manager, or even a gung-ho on-site supervisor who is excited about civility training, good luck selling it to the top brass if you (or they) are defining it as *nice to have* skills.

The fact is, words matter. And so, to ensure people recognize civility training as a real solution, I have found it helpful to define the term civility in a way that expands the thoughts and emotions that using the word typically conjures.

Civility must be defined in a way that is comprehensive enough to make people think differently. And, at the same time, it has to have immediate personal relevance for people, given whatever environment or situation they happen to be in. When a person hears the word, he or she needs to see the possibilities and imagine some of the outcomes that I have come to know are absolutely possible, for example, the long list at the beginning of this chapter. The definition has to include elements that expand it from a vague, subjective notion, to a practical, measurable concept with applications for skill development in a range of different contexts.

I am not alone in thinking that dictionary definitions of civility are not sufficient. Many civility advocates devise their own definitions of civility to make it meaningful for their specific application. As examples:

Gary Burgess, PhD, and Heidi Burgess, PhD Codirectors, Conflict Research Consortium, University of Colorado state,

> [...]Clearly, civility has to mean something more than mere politeness. The movement will have accomplished little if all it does is get people to say, 'Excuse me please,' while they (figuratively) stab you in the back. Civility also cannot mean 'roll over and play dead.' People need to be able to raise tough questions and present their cases when they feel their vital interests are being threatened. A civil society cannot avoid tough, but important issues,

simply because they are unpleasant to address. There must also be more to civility than a scrupulous adherence to the laws governing public-policy decision making...In our work at the University of Colorado's Conflict Research Consortium, we have been developing an approach which we call 'constructive confrontation.' This approach combines an understanding of conflict processes, dispute resolution, and advocacy strategies to help disputants better advance their interests. In addition to explaining why the politeness embodied in conventional definitions of 'civility' is important, we also identify a number of other areas in which adversaries, decision makers, and those caught in the middle can work individually and collectively to increase the constructiveness of public debate....

Tomas Spath and Cassandra Dahnke, Founders of the Institute for Civility in Government state, "Civility is claiming and caring for one's identity, needs and beliefs without degrading someone else's in the process." On the Institute's webpage, you will find a notation explaining the definition:

Civility is about more than just politeness, although politeness is a necessary first step. It is about disagreeing without disrespect, seeking common ground as a starting point for dialogue about differences, listening past one's preconceptions, and teaching others to do the same. Civility is the hard work of staying present even with those with whom we have deep-rooted and fierce disagreements. It is political in the sense that it is a necessary prerequisite for civic action. But it is political, too, in the sense that it is about negotiating interpersonal power such that everyone's voice is heard, and nobody's is ignored. And civility begins with us.

Dr. Pier Forni, Johns Hopkins, considered the leading U.S. researcher and author on civility,

Building on the notion of 'civilitas,' here is a possible definition of civility for our times: The civil person is someone who cares for his or her community and who looks at others with a benevolent disposition rooted in the belief that their claim to well-being and happiness is as valid as his or her own. More Americans are discerning with increasing clarity the connections between civility and ethics, civility and health, and civility and quality of life. In fact a consensus is developing around the notion that a vigorous civility is necessary for the survival of society as we know it.

According to Stephen L. Carter, author of *Civility: Manners, Morals, and the Etiquette of Democracy*, "Civility is the sum of the many sacrifices we are called to make for the sake of living together."

Dr. Cindy Clark, a Professor at Boise State who co-developed the Organizational Civility Scale® defines civility as, "Authentic respect for others requiring time, presence, engagement, and an intention to seek common ground."

And, from Kent Roberts and Jay Newman, cofounders of The National Civility Center, a not-for-profit organization established in 2000 to help people make their communities better places to live, "Civility build on the Golden Rule: Always treat others as you would like to be treated. When true civil dialogue takes place, a high-minded, self-sacrificing behavior often emerges. Those simple building blocks create positive relationships and raise levels of trust between people and institutions. And without trust, nothing of value can happen."

As you can see in reviewing these examples, there are some reoccurring themes threaded through the definitions. And, while politeness and courtesy are included in most them, they are not the focus. Instead, the impact of civility is highlighted, references to: living together, creating positive relationships, building trust, well-being and happiness, taking responsibility, valuing worth and dignity, staying present, seeking common ground, starting point for dialogue, and constructive confrontation.

It is this same end in mind approach that we used at Civility Experts Worldwide when we worked to define the term. Some of the considerations we applied in devising our definition were: the definition would have practical applications for workplaces, generally, but that could be expanded or adapted to individual and/or specific workplaces as well.

Because we have affiliates all over the world, we needed to have a definition that would be meaningful when translated and that would resonate with our affiliates, regardless of what culture they represented. We needed a definition that could inform our training and tie in to what we had come to understand as skills that underpinned overall civility competencies. We wanted to build on—and in some small way, offer tribute—to the good work of civility experts who had inspired and mentored us. For example, when I first started my civility journey, works by Dr. Pier Forni, Dr. Karl Albrecht, and Benet Davetian were top of my reading list. We wanted the definition to reflect our own personal values so that we could truly buy in and feel confident and comfortable that in choosing civility as our work, we could actually live our values.

Civility Experts Worldwide Definition of Civility

At Civility Experts Worldwide, we define civility as:

> A conscious awareness of the impact of one's thoughts, actions, words and intentions on others; combined with;
> A continuous acknowledgement of one's responsibility to ease the experience of others (e.g., through restraint, kindness, non-judgment, respect, and courtesy); and
> A consistent effort to adopt and exhibit civil behavior as a non-negotiable point of one's character.

In our definition, conscious awareness is intended to make the point that it is not enough to extend courtesy out of habit, and it is not a good enough excuse when you do not extend appropriate consideration to say you were not aware, or were not paying attention. When we are conscious of the impact of our thoughts and words and actions, when we focus and attend to our surroundings, we are reminded that we have the power to impact people and situations and communications. In attending, we become thoughtful, and when we are thoughtful, we become thinkers, As Dr. Forni says in his latest book, *The Thinking Life-How to Thrive in the Age of Distraction*, "You are thoughtful if you are a thinker, but you are also thoughtful if you are considerate. To be considerate you need first of all, to pay attention to other people…you need to think about them and their well-being." Very few could argue that we do not live in an age of distraction. As such, that someone is deliberate in thinking before he or she acts or speaks, and that he or she then intentionally chooses a civil action, even when it may not be comfortable, cost-free, or convenient to do so, speaks volumes about that individual's character. Sadly, many of us are too caught up in ourselves to look up and attend to what is going on around us. And, when we do have occasion to look up, many of us are distracted and often not present to, or caring about anyone. To me, the breadth of incivility we experience every day is a good indication that thinking is not as common a pursuit as it once was.

When we talk about a "continuous acknowledgement of one's responsibility," we are referencing ethics and the inherent human dignity of others. Easing the experience of others echoes the do no harm principle that has been the bedrock of Eastern and Western religious traditions alike. In the workplace, this responsibility ties to accountability and includes obligations related to common courtesy, nonjudgment, and restraint, regardless of whether they are written into a job description or code of conduct.

Consistent effort relates to the point that when standards are at issue, as happens in most workplaces, being civil some of the time is not enough. Civility must be an everyday, all-day endeavor. This is essential to building trust. Choosing civility has to become our default thinking pattern. It must become imbedded in the workplace culture such that it becomes a key part of the character of the organization and a reflection of the character of the people who make up the organization. This element of our definition also suggests the ongoing hard work and commitment that is required to build a culture of civility. Truly, if it were easy to choose civility, wouldn't everyone would be doing it?

From a leadership and/or individual perspective, choosing civility means that when interacting with others, you do so with purpose and have an understanding of the value of the written and unwritten rules beyond mere social requirements. For example, encouraging all levels of the work team to sit together at lunch and breaks is not so much about acting civilized, as it is about choosing to take time to be together, to laugh, to tell stories, to connect in some small way.

Outcomes of Civility Training

The outcomes of civility initiatives generally and civility training specifically are as follows:

- Increased retention
- Greater individual and organizational adaptive capacity
- Employee autonomy
- Individual skills mastery and increased confidence
- More effective goal-setting
- Better alignment of daily activity with organizational goals
- More accountability
- Greater consistency in service delivery
- Increased respect in the workplace
- More frequent exhibition of common courtesies
- Generalized reciprocity
- More civil discourse
- Increased acceptance of diversity
- Greater team orientation
- More collaboration
- Increased innovation
- Improved thinking skills
- Improved self-respect
- More self-directed learning
- Improved culture of learning
- Greater change readiness
- Improved engagement
- Higher understanding of shared purpose
- Increased trust
- More responsibility-taking
- Higher self-rated happy at work scores
- Employee hardiness
- Increased psychological safety
- Better stress management
- Increased exercising of restraint
- Improved morale
- More efficient communication

You will see that having a clear definition of civility for application in a specific context will help get the change makers and leadership on board. The definition will also set the groundwork for achieving some of those positive outcomes we introduced you to at the beginning of this chapter.

Before we move on to how to assess and how to build civility in your workplace, let us briefly discuss civility relative to some other terms and concepts that are closely related and will likely come up in your civility conversations and training.

What Is the Difference Between Civility, Etiquette, Courtesy, and Manners?

Etiquette guidelines, which incorporate manners, represent the rules or conventions that apply to a situation, a time, a culture, or a country. Courtesy represents a demeanor, an attitude of respectful or reverence for a specific set of social rules. And, manners are the polite behaviors we use to express courtesy. Manners are frequently dictated by etiquette rules and relate to what is expected for a given situation, for example, wedding etiquette, funeral etiquette, dining etiquette, golf etiquette. I believe you do not have to know or follow etiquette rules to be civil. And, following prescribed social conventions out of some sense of obligation, or being courteous just because you are directed to do so by some person or circumstance, *without* some measure of understanding and good intention, is not nearly the same as choosing and practicing civility.

Put simply, courtesy is about convention, and civility is about conscience.

Etiquette helps us get along better together, and manners foster social decorum, so there is that. But, in the grand scheme of things, I personally care more about you paying me some focused attention and making me feel valued in your presence, than I care about which fork you use or whether you wear white after Labor Day. Regarding the relationship between incivility and rudeness, rudeness is certainly uncivil, but it relates more to a behavior that breaches a known rule. Incivility is more about behaviors that breach values and/or ethics and these are, so incivility incorporates both behavior and intention or attitude.

In *Choose Civility*, Dr. Forni, describes rudeness as follows:

- Rudeness diminishes and demeans others. It is taking without giving.
- Unfocused rudeness is done in obliviousness.
- Focused rudeness is mean-spirited. Continued focused rudeness can be bullying or harassment.
- Rudeness damages others by creating stress, eroding self-esteem, creating problems in relationships, making things difficult at work, and escalating into violence. Rudeness leaves us vulnerable to self-doubt and anxiety. People who are treated rudely can withdraw or become aggressive.

As a side note, *protocol* is an assigned process, approach, or procedure, for a specific context. Protocol is often dictated by regulated or written rules, and these are more rigid than etiquette rules, which really function as guidelines. Protocol is to be followed without deviation, sometimes for safety reasons, for example, military protocol or medical protocol. But, when following etiquette guidelines, you are expected to consider the circumstances, and sometimes, it is appropriate to break the rule. As an example, in North America, it is considered good business etiquette to extend your hand for a handshake when you first meet someone. However, if you note that a person has his or her hands full, or that he or she does not appear comfortable with a handshake, you would be expected to know that breaking the etiquette rule to ensure the other party is not embarrassed or uncomfortable is the courteous thing to do.

How Does Civility Relate to Values?

Civility is a values proposition. Choosing civility means that civility (defined however you prefer) represents a personal principle or value. A value is a standard or code that we, as individuals and/or as a collective (may be a family and organization or a community), live by. Our values impact how we make decisions, and how we determine what is important to us. When groups of individuals share the same core values, those values create the character or culture of a family, an organization, and even a nation. When you do not have clearly defined values, it is difficult to establish personal standards, and so it is easier to choose popular actions based on convenience rather than choose civility based on conscience. The end result is incivility.

Is Civility not the Same Thing as Character?

Allan Greenspan, Former Chairman, U.S. Federal Reserve said, "Rules cannot take the place of character." I agree. Following this line of thought, if you are defining civility as etiquette, following these mannerly rules is not the same as having character. Choosing the right action, weighing the potential impact of choices against one's own values, and being accountable for the outcomes of those choices are what build a character. And, it is the character that distinguishes mannerly actions from civility.

In his new book *Return on Character*, Fred Kiel, defines character as "An individual's unique combination of beliefs and character habits that motivate and shape how he or she relates to others. Our character is defined by out behavior- the way we treat others is character in action." Kiel goes on to suggest that there are four keystone character habits: integrity, responsibility, forgiveness, and compassion. According to Kiel, these character habits are the direct expression of our innate moral intuitions. These intuitions not only make us uniquely human, but the habitual demonstration of the principles they foster is essential to the kind of strong, principled character we associate with what he calls *Virtuoso* leadership.

Abraham Lincoln said, "Reputation is the shadow. Character is the tree." Civility, as an element of character, is what compels you to do the right thing just because it is right to do what is right. This belief is an aspect of your true self, part of your character, whereas manners can easily and often be exhibited simply as a means of sending a positive impression or appearing to be good.

How Is Being Civil Different From Showing Respect?

In my mind, being civil is not exactly the same as showing respect. However, the two are very closely related. The difference is most easily explained in saying that civility is perceived as a gesture or communication that is meaningful to someone else. And so, to be civil, there is usually some consciousness or awareness of what the other person might need or want. And so, to be civil is usually something intentional. For example, in speaking of civility, many people have adopted what is described as "The Platinum Rule" over "The Golden Rule." Where the Golden Rule says that we should do unto others as we would have done to us (this means assuming others want what we want or expect), the Platinum Rule, according to Tony Alessandra, says that we should treat someone as he or she wishes to be treated. To follow the Platinum Rule, you have to set assumptions aside and consider the perspectives of others. In doing so, you adopt an *other-focus*, and in this way, I believe that to be civil, one necessarily conveys a service orientation. I believe that showing respect is a way of honoring someone's humanness. And, you should not have to know that person or share his or her perspective, or understand what he or she wants or believes or feels, to respect him or her. Respect is something that should be automatically, spontaneously, and easily given. Put simply, respect is something you feel toward someone, and this is often unconscious. Where civility is something you consciously choose—this is one of the reasons I believe you can teach civility, but it is much harder to teach respect. Sure I can explain what respect looks like, but that is now the same as teaching how to truly feel respect in one's heart. This requires setting aside bias and prejudice for example, and this can be a difficult endeavor.

The reality is that someone could perceive him or herself as being treated in a respectful way or see him or herself having been treated civilly merely as a result of someone else extending a courtesy—and this can be a mistake. In actuality, that someone says something kind or does what the rules say he or she should do, for example, gives a gift, sends a thank you note, and shows up on time, does not mean that this person is civil. And, it does not necessarily mean that the person respects us. Frequently, people can have respect for the rules and so exhibit them, and still not have respect for the people they are following the rules for.

Respectfulness is absolutely a part of being civil. When a person is truly civil, he or she understands that respect is something that should be given with no expectation of return. Respecting others just because they are human, and in being human they are deserving of our respect, and deserving of their dignity, shows a civil attitude. This civil attitude is an indication that we are not judgmental, and that we recognize everyone as equal. That I would say, or think, that someone needs to earn my respect for example, suggests that I am not civil. I would argue that often when we say we do not respect someone, we actually mean we do not trust him or her. Similarly, when someone does not seem to give us respect without measuring our value, we do not trust that person.

When you explain respect as aforementioned, it is easier to understand how someone could respect the rules, but not trust the person making them. Or, how you can respect someone on a basic human level, and at the same time, be discourteous (break a social rule) to that person. I can respect myself, but not trust myself. I can respect you, but not trust you.

I can be civil, that is, choose not to judge you, and be courteous (be polite) and respect you (accept you for who you are and treat you as equal), and at the same time, have different views, live differently, and potentially behave in a way that you perceive as rude. Maybe you call this rudeness disrespectful, and maybe you do not trust me as a result of it. But, even when you are rude, while I do not appreciate your behavior, I can still respect you as a person. And, if you are civil, you will still respect me too, even if you behave rudely toward me. The fact that I breached a rule that you adhere value to does not make me an uncivil person. Rude, maybe. Impolite, sure. But, not uncivil.

What Is the Difference Between Civility and Ethics?

Mostly, everyone in the civility training field would agree that civility is closely aligned with ethics. But, this debate can get messy. Much depends on how you define ethics. Another example of how words matter. Dr. Forni, in *Choosing Civility*, developed four principles about civility: (1) civility is complex; (2) civility is good; (3) whatever civility might be, it has to do with courtesy, politeness, and manners; and (4) civility belongs in the realm of ethics. And, he goes on to say,

> What gives true civility depth and importance is, first of all, its connection with ethics. Just look at the Principle of Respect for Persons, a cornerstone of all ethical systems known to history.

It states that we are to treat others as ends in themselves rather than as means for the furthering of our personal advantage. In other words, our behavior must be informed by empathy.

In his book, *Ethical Intelligence*, Bruce Weinstein describes five simple principles that help us make the best decisions—no matter who is looking at a problem. I am hard pressed to think of a civility training session where some or all of these terms did not enter in, they are:

- Do no harm
- Make things better
- Respect others
- Be fair
- Be loving

Weinstein suggests that we know these principles already, they are the basis of both religious traditions and secular societies, and they are tremendously hard to live by. Further, he states, "...all five principles mentioned above provide excellent guidelines for making the best possible decisions in every area of your life. These principles have legal, financial, and psychological implications; *but they* are first and foremost principles of ethics and they form the core of what I call *ethical intelligence*." There is no question that alignment between civility and these five principles, for example, Mr. Weinstein states in his book that *do no harm* is largely a principle of restraint. And, restraint is a notion that comes up frequently in civility conversations. For example, Dr. Pier Forni, considered one of the leading scholars in the field, suggests that the three key tenants of civility are: respect, restraint, and responsibility.

Additionally, when discussing Principle #3—respect others, Weinstein explains that,

> ...respect is not just a matter of etiquette. Rude or offensive behavior is a breach of etiquette. But behavior that is harmful or violates another person's rights is a breach of ethics. Ethically intelligent people show respect in the deeper sense by honoring the values, preferences, and, most important, the rights of others.... Rights

speak to the inherent dignity inhuman beings…these rights never change. They are the basis of legal rights but they exist even when not codified by law.

In my view, ethics relate to what is right and wrong, independent of what regulations, workplace codes of conduct, or legislations might state. This is where conversations about moral conduct and human rights begin. While some people have an absolute personal line in terms of what is ethical, there are many influencing, and ever-changing, factors and, sometimes, culture, religion, law, and context come into play. Ongoing debates about abortion, assisted suicide, and human cloning, for example, represent ethical questions that are not likely to be resolved any time soon. Over the years I have come to understand that what is civil is frequently ethical, but not always. And, being ethical does not always include being civil, at least not the way I define it. It occurs to me that in determining what is ethical, we look inward and rely on conscience. Whereas, in determining what is civil, we tend to look outward and rely more on the expectations of our community and society. I am also inclined to say that civility is the *kind* thing—regardless of the rules, whereas ethics is the *right* thing—with a direct correlation to inherent human dignity (for some people, this dignity and rights extend to all living things). With regard to the questions about whether I think rampant permissive incivility enables moral turpitude—my view is that where there is no conscience, there are likely no ethics, and so it is a lack of conscience that enables evil in the form of moral turpitude and not permissible incivility that causes it.

Civility and Emotional Intelligence

In 1995, Daniel Goleman wrote a book on emotional intelligence or EQ. Ground-breaking at the time, Goleman suggested that the ability to discern how you and others feel (and what might be the root cause of those feelings) regardless of what you may be outwardly presenting to the world, for example, through your demeanor or body language, was essential to building relationships and a key component of success. The essential premise of EQ is that, to be successful requires the effective awareness, control and management of one's own emotions, and those of other people. According to Goleman, EQ embraces two aspects of intelligence:

- Understanding yourself, your goals, intentions, responses, behavior, and all.
- Understanding others and their feelings.

While I agree with the esteemed Dr. Goleman that there is tremendous value in knowing oneself, and that having the ability to be aware of, control, and manage one's own emotions and the emotions of others, I am not convinced that building emotional intelligence is the most important intelligence for workplace.

As was included in our definition of civility, awareness of the impact of your thoughts, feelings, words, and actions on others is important for civility in the workplace. My opinion is that focus on internal drivers and feelings end up putting more importance on the intent and motivation for doing and feeling, and this is contrary to the other focus we need to build civility in the workplace. Further, my view is that this self-development and reflective work is what the individual should take responsibility for, independent of the workplace. I do not believe that beyond the regulated psychological safety elements, it should be the employer's responsibility to delve into each employees' emotional issues and sort out what makes him or her tick. As an employer, this is not where I would put my training dollars. Some exceptions would be if we are working in a sector where empathy and emotion are an important part of the job, such as healthcare or childcare. In Chapter 7, we are going to discuss how another type of intelligence—social intelligence—may, in fact, be more useful in building civility as a core competence.

Civility and Positive Psychology

There has been a lot of buzz lately about *positive psychology*. Positive psychology is the study of happiness. *Martin Seligman* and *Mihaly Csikszentmihalyi* describe this term in the following way: "We believe that a psychology of positive human functioning will arise that achieves a scientific understanding and effective interventions to build thriving in individuals, families, and communities." Positive psychology is tied to civility, in that the research shows positive psychology promotes character development, positive interactions, stress reduction, gratitude, and altruism. These outcomes echo what we see when there is a culture of civility imbedded in workplaces. A related term is *positive intelligence*. Positive intelligence can be measured as the percentage of the time your mind works for you instead of against you. There is a tug of war constantly raging inside your mind between your saboteurs—the mental patterns that sabotage your success and well-being—and your sage—the mental patterns that serve positive intelligence is the groundbreaking new science and practice of stress-free peak performance. The scientific foundation of positive intelligence is a synthesis of breakthrough break through original research by Shirzad Chamine. The greatest differentiators in performance and achievement are *soft skills* and mindset, such as emotional intelligence. Positive intelligence builds on the principles of emotional intelligence and goes a step further by addressing a missing component of emotional intelligence training—mastery over the internal saboteurs. Recent scientific studies have established that positive intelligence is a significant determinant of how much of your potential for both happiness and professional success you actually achieve. Positive intelligence has been directly linked to a wide range of measurable benefits:

- Sales people sell 37 percent more.
- Teams perform 31 percent better with high PQ leaders.
- Creative output increases three times.
- People live as much as 10 years longer.

Civility and Being Nice or Being Kind

Renowned Lebanese Poet Kahil Gilbran said, "Tenderness and kindness are not signs of weakness and despair, but manifestations of strength and resolution." Based on the Civility Experts Worldwide definition of civility, kindness is one of the ways we can ease the experience of others. Kindness often takes planning, and sometimes discipline. Additionally, being kind frequently requires restraint. Further, I believe kindness is a precursor to generosity. True, heartfelt, spontaneous kindness is given as civility, should be with no expectation of return. Getting to the point where you can give your time, money, energy, or attention, without monitoring the cost of doing same is very difficult to achieve.

It is not easy to be kind, especially when you are surrounded by unkind. Indeed, these days, choosing civility takes courage, strength, and resolution.

In her book, *Saving Civility; 52 Ways to Tame Rude, Crude and Attitude for a Polite Planet*, Sarah Hacala describes kindness as, "...charity, generosity, compassion, and empathy...as it applies to good behavior, it is an almost inclusive antidote to disrespect, inconsideration and rudeness. If we were simply kind to everyone, a host of other negative behaviors would fall by the wayside".

Recommended Homework

Respectful Workplace Policy

Training activity purpose: To make your own respectful workplace policy.

Application: As soon as you are comfortable that you understand the importance of civility in the workplace, please complete this exercise. The goal is to envision a kind of *perfect world* scenario, which can then be boiled down, so to speak, into a more realistic and actionable plan.

Outcome: A draft workplace policy built by consensus, applying concepts learned to date.

From the Field—Tools you can use: Sample template for a respectful workplace policy created by the Petroleum Human Resources Council of Canada http://petrohrsc.ca/media/15025/Respectfulpercent20Workplac epercent20Policypercent20Template.pdf.

Respectful workplace policy template: This template on respectful workplace policy can be used by any company operating within Canada to prevent and deal with discrimination and harassment in the workplace.

Aside from adopting this policy, companies are encouraged to provide education and training for their employees and contractors, whenever applicable, on the following key topics: human rights in the workplace, managing diversity, and the company's respectful workplace policy and procedures.

Test Yourself

1. Civility must be defined in a way that:
   a. Makes people think differently
   b. Distinguishes between civility and ethics
   c. Translates easily to other languages
2. According to Goleman, emotional intelligence includes how many aspects of intelligence:
   a. Three
   b. Six
   c. Two
3. The three aspects of Civility Experts Inc. definition of civility are:
   a. Character, confidence, attention
   b. Effort, consistency, character
   c. Awareness, acknowledgment, effort

CHAPTER 3

The Business Case for Civility

You to the boss: Boss, what would you do with 30 percent more revenue?

Boss to you: I could do a lot, what do you know that I do not?

You to the boss: I know that companies that openly promote civil communication among employees earn 30 percent more revenue than competitors[1].

Boss to you: Really? So tell me again...why are we not doing civility training?

You to the boss: Just say when boss, should not be too hard a sell the idea of civility training to the team, as 67 percent of the employees who responded to a Civility in America poll said they believe there is a strong need for civility training[2].

Boss to you: Offering training that 67 percent of employees say they want, as a means of achieving 30 percent more revenue...seems like a no brainer to me, let us get started!

Are *you* convinced that civility is important to business yet? After reviewing the Introduction and chapters 1 and 2, you should have a clearer idea of what civility is and, hopefully, you agree with the research showing that most organizations are dealing with incivility in the workplace to some degree. By the end this chapter, we hope you will also see that based

---

[1] Shandwick, Weber, and Tate, Powell. 2011. "Civility in America 2011." http://webershandwick.com/uploads/news/files/Civility_in_America_2011.pdf

[2] Ibid.

on the business case, implementing a civility initiative, the workplace is more than just a good idea. "A Civility Initiative is a change imperative for organizations that want to succeed in the new world of work." Further, we want to provide you with the information you need to persuade your leadership and teams to choose civility and support your workplace civility initiative. Approaching civility at work as a change initiative is one way to manage the impact of incivility in the workplace and change your overall organizational culture for the better.

It is never too soon to start working on your own personal definition of civility. Although you may not be able to finalize a definition, the goal is that you would be able to at least describe for the naysayers and skeptical decision makers what civility is *not*. If you are able to at least define what civility means to you personally, you can fall back on this definition as a way of illustrating to others what civility looks like in practice, as well as what it means relative to other commonly associated terms such as manners, ethics, courtesy, morals, and so on.

If you have a personal interest in civility but are not quite ready to introduce the concept in your workplace, you might benefit from the *I Choose Civility: Steps to Adopting Civility as a Core Personal Value* worksheet in Chapter 11, Tools You Can Use.

If you are a decision maker who has reviewed that long list of potential positive outcomes at the beginning of Chapter 2, you may already be considering civility training for your organization. In this case, extracting facts and stats and other information provided in this chapter will help you present the business case for civility training to your team.

Strategies for Persuading Others That Civility at Work Is Important

Whatever your role is in your organization, unless you have access to a pot of unallocated funds that you are free to spend on whatever training you can get your hands on, you will need to persuade others to get on board. There are two issues to consider in achieving this:

1. You have to figure out how to get over the "civility = manners = soft skills, and soft skills are nice to have but not necessary skills" hurdle. Even if we take manners out of the equation, civility still equals soft

skills to most people, and this can be problematic when it comes to training decisions and budgeting.

2. You have to know your audience. What will convince your team that civility training is worthwhile? Will it be a focus on costs, benefits, or consequences? Because I feel it is actually contrary to civility to engage in ongoing conversations about negative behavior, my approach to making the business case is *always to focus on the benefits* and the research verifying the positive impacts of civility. Before we get into the business case for civility training, some assertions we are making in presenting the evidence that civility training works.

Assertions made when presenting evidence that civility training works are as follows:

- Civility is...
  1. A conscious awareness of the impact of one's thoughts, actions, words, and intentions on others; combined with;
  2. A continuous acknowledgment of one's responsibility to ease the experience of others (e.g., through restraint, kindness, non-judgment, respect, and courtesy); and
  3. A consistent effort to adopt and exhibit civil behavior as a non-negotiable point of one's character.
     (This is the Civility Experts Worldwide definition)
- On the surface, civility is perceived to be largely attitudinal, but as per the aforementioned definition, is also understood to encompass a range of *soft* skills
- Soft skills are proving to be equally, or more important than, technical skills (this is especially true in the new world of work—we talk about this in Chapter 4)
- Soft skills—as per Han's definitions—enable individuals to effectively apply technical skills, and exhibiting soft skills requires some technical abilities; soft and technical skills are not necessarily useful independent of each other

Note: If you are using a different definition of civility than the one presented earlier, consider whether your definition includes a *soft skills* element. If not, aspects of the *Civility Culture Compass*® may not work for you.

What Are Soft Skills?

Soft skills can be described as a cluster of personal qualities that include things like:

- Approach to communication
- Cooperative attitude
- Personal habits
- Emotional intelligence
- Social style, and so on

These are nontechnical skills, sometimes intangible, and often hard to measure because they tend to be more related to willingness, attitude, personality, and social intelligence than they are related to physical ability or intellectual capacity.

You will see in Chapter 7 when we talk about competencies that support a culture of civility that I believe there are four measurable skills that as a collective make up what we at Civility Experts refer to as the "Civility Competency Matrix®." These skills support an individual's ability to exhibit civility generally, but on the job specifically.

Lei Han, Stanford engineer, Wharton MBA, offers clarification on what soft skills are versus people skills, and what she calls *tribal* skills. For a skill to be considered soft, it needs to have three characteristics:

1. *Rules for mastering this skill are not black and white*: Unlike hard skills, like math, where the rule for doing it perfectly is always the same, how effective you are at a soft skill changes depends on your emotional state, external circumstance, and the type of people you interact with.
2. *This skill is portable and valuable* to any job or career: Because soft skills are about your inner strength and interpersonal effectiveness, as long as you work with people, these skills are valuable to your career.
3. Mastering this skill is an ongoing journey: You can reach a level of competency in it, but you can always encounter new situations or people who will test your soft skills and push you to learn more.

Han's Soft Skills List Part A: Self-Management Skills

Self-management skills address how you perceive yourself and others, manage your emotions, and react to adverse situations. Only when you build an inner excellence can you have a strong mental and emotional foundation to succeed in your career.

1. Growth mindset: Looking at any situation, especially difficult ones, as an opportunity for you to learn, grow, and change for the better. Focusing your attention on improving yourself, instead of changing others or blaming anyone.

2. Self-awareness: Knowing and understanding what drives, angers, motivates, embarrasses, frustrates, and inspires you. Being able to observe yourself objectively in a difficult situation and understand how your perceptions of yourself, others, and the situation are driving your actions.

3. Emotion regulation: Being able to manage your emotions, especially negative ones, at work (e.g., anger, frustration, embarrassment) so that you can think clearly and objectively, and act accordingly.

4. Self-confidence: Believing in yourself and your ability to accomplish anything. Knowing that all you need is within you now. "Those who believe in themselves have access to unlimited power"—wisdom from Kung Fu Panda.

5. Stress management: Being able to stay healthy, calm, and balanced in any challenging situations. Knowing how to reduce your stress level will increase your productivity, prepare you for new challenges, and support your physical and emotional health, all of which you need for a fulfilling, successful career.

6. Resilience: Being able to bounce back after a disappointment or set back, big or small, and continue to move onward and upward.

7. Skills to forgive and forget: Being able to forgive yourself for making a mistake, forgive others that wronged you, and move on without *mental or emotional baggage*. Freeing your mind from the past so that you can focus 100 percent of your mental energy on your short- and long-term career goals.

8. Persistence and perseverance: Being able to maintain the same energy and dedication in your effort to learn, do, and achieve in your career despite difficulties, failures, and oppositions.

9. Patience: Being able to step back in a seemingly rushed or crisis situation so that you can think clearly and take action that fulfills your long-term goals.

10. Perceptiveness: Giving attention and understanding to the unspoken cues and underlying nuance of other people's communication and actions. Oftentimes, we are too busy thinking about ourselves and what we are saying, so we leave little room to watch and understand others' action and intentions. If you misinterpret others' intention, you can easily encounter difficulties dealing with people and not even know why. (FYI, you will note in Chapter 7 under the Social Intelligence section that Han's self-management skills make up much of what we reference as *social style*, and they are inter-woven with *social radar*.)

Han's Soft Skills List Part B: People Skills

People skills address how to best interact and work with others so that you can build meaningful work relationships, influence others' perception of you and your work, and motivate their actions. I have split them into two sections—conventional and tribal.

People skills subgroup 1: Conventional skills: List of people skills you can find in most job descriptions, and you will be assessed on some or all of these in your performance reviews depending on your level. (FYI, you will note in Chapter 7 when we reference the *written rules and social knowledge*, many of the skills on Han's conventional skills list require high social radar, and are influenced by etiquette and contextual rules.)

1. Communication skills: Being able to actively listen to others and articulate your ideas in writing and verbally to any audience in a way where you are heard and you achieve the goals you intended with that communication.

2. Teamwork skills: Being able to work effectively with anyone with different skill sets, personalities, work styles, or motivation levels to achieve a better team result.

3. Interpersonal relationship skills: Effective at building trust, finding common ground, having empathy, and ultimately building strong relationships with people at work and in your network. This skill is closely related to communication skills. As Maya Angelou said "I have learned people will forget what you said. People will forget what you did, but people will never forget how you make them feel."

4. Presentation skills: Effectively presenting your work results and ideas formally to an audience that captivates their attention, engages their input, and motivates them to act in accordance to your desired outcome. While presentation skills are a form of communication skills, they are listed separately, given that the ability to present plays a huge role in any business profession, especially as you move up in your career.

5. Meeting management skills: Leading a meeting to efficiently and effectively reach productive results. At least 50 percent of the meetings today are a waste of time.

6. Facilitating skills: Being able to coordinate and solicit well-represented opinions and feedback from a group with diverse perspectives to reach a common, best solution.

7. Selling skills—Building buy-in to an idea, a decision, an action, a product, or a service. This is not just for people in sales.

8. Management skills: Creating and motivating a high-performing team with people of varied skills, personalities, motivations, and work styles.

9. Leadership skills: Defining and communicating vision and ideas that inspire others to follow with commitment and dedication.

10. Mentoring or coaching skills: Providing constructive wisdom, guidance, and/or feedback that can help others further their career development.

People skills subgroup 2: *Tribal* skills: List of people skills that you will not typically find in job descriptions. They are also important to your career success. Han calls them *tribal* because they are more *insider knowledge* that you gain from work experience or from mentors. Some people can go through their entire career and not be aware of some of these skills.

(FYI, you will see in Chapter 7 in the Social Intelligence section that Han's tribal skills are in large part what we reference as *the unwritten rules* component of social knowledge.)

11. Managing upward: Proactively managing your relationship with your boss, his or her expectations of your work, and his or her perception of your performance. Whether you are challenged, given opportunities, or recognized at work heavily depends on your ability to communicate, manage expectations, and build a good relationship with your boss.

12. Self-promotion skills: Proactively and subtly promoting your skills and work results to people of power or influence in your organization and network. It is not enough that your boss knows you do great work. You need to subtly build your reputation with all key people who can influence your performance review. This is because hard work alone does not guarantee success.

13. Skills in dealing with difficult personalities: Being able to achieve the work result needed while working with someone whom you find difficult.

14. Skills in dealing with difficult or unexpected situations: Being able to stay calm and still are effective when faced with an unexpected or difficult situation. This includes being able to think on your feet and articulate thoughts in an organized manner even when you are not prepared for the discussion or situation you are in.

15. Savvy in handling office politics: Being able to understand and proactively deal with the unspoken nuances of office and people dynamics so that you can protect yourself from unfairness as well as further your career. Office politics are a fact of life. If you do not choose to play, they can play you.

16. Influence or persuasion skills: Being able to influence perspectives or decision making, but still have the people you influence think they made up their own minds.

17. Negotiation skills: Being able to understand the other side's motivations and leverage and reach a win–win resolution that you find

favorably satisfies both sides and maintains relationships for future interactions.

18. Networking skills: Being able to be interesting and interested in business conversations that motivate people to want to be in your network. The bigger and stronger the network you have, the more easily you can get things done (e.g., find a job, get advice, find business partners, find customers)[3].

As you can see upon reviewing Ms. Han's definitions, every single soft skill, whether indicated as self-managed, people, or tribal includes one or more aspects of conscious awareness, consistent acknowledgement, and consistency—the three key elements in our definition of civility. We will get into this in more depth in Chapter 7, Competencies that Support Civility in the Workplace. A checklist of Ms. Han's soft skills with the civility definition elements indicated in includes in Chapter 9, Tools You Can Use.

What the Research Shows About Soft Skills Relative to Technical Skills

Research carried out by the Carnegie Institute of Technology shows that 85 percent of your financial success is because of skills in *human engineering*, your personality, and ability to communicate, negotiate, and lead. Shockingly, only 15 percent is because of technical knowledge[4].

Dr. John Fleenor of the Center for Creative Leadership explains that the CEO's *soft* skills make all the difference. To be successful, individuals must be good listeners, consensus builders, team players, and

---

[3] Lei H. 2017. "Soft Skills List - 28 Skills to Working Smart." *Soft Skills - Ask a Wharton MBA,* May 9, 2017, https://bemycareercoach.com/soft-skills/list-soft-skills.html

[4] Charles R. Mann. 1918. "A Study of Engineering Education." *The Carnegie Foundation for the Advancement of Teaching,* http://web.mit.edu/~jwk/www/docs/Mann%201918%20Study_of_Engineering_Educ.pdf.

empathizers. Hence, to climb the corporate ladder quickly, it is essential for executives to possess more of soft skills and less of hard skills. We can compare soft skills with emotional intelligence quotient (EQ) and hard skills with intelligence quotient (IQ). Succinctly, soft skills are twice as important as IQ or technical skills for the success of senior executives. Studies have shown that individuals with high emotional quotient are highly appreciated in the workplace and they tend to grow rapidly in the corporate ladder[5].

To Daniel Goleman, author of several books on relational intelligence, soft skills are a combination of competencies that contribute to a person's ability to manage him or herself and relate to other people. These are the skills, abilities, and traits concerning the personality, attitude, and behavior of a person. They are the human skills that make a huge difference for your professional success. They are needed for good leaders to become great leaders. By contrast, hard skills are about your technical competence and domain expertise. Sometimes, soft skills are equated with teamwork, while hard skills with execution. Hence, executives must proportionately blend the soft and hard skills with leadership to excel as successful leaders. However, as they gain more experience, they need more of soft skills because they work less on their hard skills and more on interpersonal skills. They are mostly into visioning, troubleshooting, and managing several stakeholders, which demands soft skills and leadership skills[6].

Nobel Prize-winning psychologist Daniel Kahneman found that *people* would *rather do business with* a *person they like* and trust rather than *someone they* do not, even if the person they do not like is offering a better price or higher-quality product[7]. The ability to build trust is largely based on soft skills.

---

[5] Leading Effectively Staff, "Press Releases Archives," Center for Creative Leadership, http://ccl.org/leadership/news/2002/softskillssurvey.aspx?pageId=694

[6] Matt, W. 2014. "Acquire Soft Skills to Fast-Track Your Career Success." *Under30CEO*, March 10, 2014, http://under30ceo.com/acquire-soft-skills-fast-track-career-success/.

[7] Daniel Kahneman, *Thinking, Fast and Slow* (New York: Farrar, Straus and Giroux, 2015).

Recommended Homework

Review the list of civility-related soft skills listed on the chart and make a personal development plan for building the three skills you self-identify as your lowest in terms of ability.

Soft Skills and Civility Checklist

This checklist is based on work by Lei Han, Stanford engineer, Wharton MBA[8] and the Civility Experts Worldwide definition of civility[9]. And, the Civility Competency Matrix[10].

If we define civility as:

- A *conscious awareness* of the impact of one's thoughts, actions, words, and intentions on others; combined with;
- A *continuous acknowledgment* of one's responsibility to ease the experience of others (e.g., through restraint, kindness, nonjudgment, respect, and courtesy); and
- A *consistent effort* to adopt and exhibit civil behavior as a non-negotiable point of one's character.

You can see how each of the soft skills identified by Lei Han includes an element of civility. How many of these soft skills are you competent in? The extent to which you can exhibit these skills could be an indication of your overall ability to exhibit civility.

Soft Skills List: People Skills

People skills address how to best interact and work with others so that you can build meaningful work relationships, influence others perception of you and your work, and motivate their actions. I have split them into two sections—conventional and tribal.

---

[8] Author Lei Han, "Soft Skills List - 28 Skills to Working Smart," Soft Skills - Ask a Wharton MBA, May 9, 2017, https://bemycareercoach.com/soft-skills/list-soft-skills.html

[9] "Home," Civility Experts Worldwide—Winnipeg Manitoba Canada, https://civilityexperts.com/

[10] Lew Bayer, Civility Experts Worldwide, 2014.

I Have This Skill (Check for Yes)	Self-Regulated Skills Han's Skill Definition	Civility Element and Link to CEW Definition
	Growth mindset – Looking at any situation, especially difficult situations, as an opportunity for you to learn, grow, and change for the better. Focusing your attention on improving yourself instead of changing others or blaming anyone.	Continuous Learning Conscious Awareness of Impact on Others
	Self-awareness –Knowing and understanding what drives, angers, motivates, embarrasses, frustrates, and inspires you. Being able to observe yourself objectively in a difficult situation and understand how your perceptions of yourself, others, and the situation are driving your actions.	Continuous Learning, Social Intelligence with elements of Emotional Intelligence Conscious Awareness of Impact on Others
	Emotion regulation –Being able to manage your emotions, especially negative ones, at work (e.g. anger, frustration, embarrassment) so you can think clearly and objectively, and act accordingly.	Thinking Skills, Personal Management Basics Conscious Awareness of Impact on Others Continuous Acknowledgement of Responsibility Consistent Effort to Exhibit Civil Behavior
	Self-confidence –Believing in yourself and your ability to accomplish anything. Knowing that all you need is within you now.	Thinking Skills Continuous Acknowledgement of Responsibility
	Stress management –Being able to stay healthy, calm, and balanced in any challenging situations. Knowing how to reduce your stress level will increase your productivity, prepare you for new challenges and supports your physical and emotional health, all of which you need for a fulfilling, successful career.	Social Intelligence, Thinking Skills, Personal Management Basics Conscious Awareness of Impact on Others Consistent Effort to Exhibit Civil Behavior
	Resilience –Being able to bounce back after a disappointment or set back, big or small, and continue to move onward and upward.	Continuous Learning, Thinking Skills Conscious Awareness of Impact on Others
	Skills to **forgive and forget** –Being able to forgive yourself for making a mistake, forgive others that wronged you, and move on without "mental or emotional baggage." Freeing your mind from the past so you can focus 100% of your mental energy on your near and long-term career goals.	Continuous learning Conscious Awareness of Impact on Others Continuous Acknowledgement of Responsibility
	Persistence and perseverance –Being able to maintain the same energy and dedication in your effort to learn, do, and achieve in your career despite difficulties, failures, and oppositions.	Thinking Skills Consistent Effort to Exhibit Civil Behavior

Figure 3.1

I Have This Skill (Check for Yes)	Self-Regulated Skills Han's Skill Definition	Civility Element and Link to CEW Definition
	Patience –Being able to step back in a seemingly rushed or crisis situation, so you can think clearly and take action that fulfills your long term goals.	Social IQ, Thinking Skills, Personal Management Basics Conscious Awareness of Impact on Others Consistent Effort to Exhibit Civil Behavior
	Perceptiveness –Giving attention and understanding to the unspoken cues and underlying nuance of other people's communication and actions. Often times, we are too busy thinking about ourselves and what we are saying, we leave little room to watch and understand others' action and intentions. If you misinterpret other's intention, you can easily encounter difficulties dealing with people and not even know why.	Social IQ Conscious Awareness of Impact on Others Continuous Acknowledgement of Responsibility

Figure 3.1 (Continued)

I Have this Skill (Check for Yes)	Self-Regulated Skills Han's Skill Definition	Civility Matrix Element and Link to CEW Definition
	Communication skills –Being able to actively listen to others and articulate your ideas in writing and verbally to any audience in a way where you are heard and you achieve the goals you intended with that communication.	Communication Skills Conscious Awareness of Impact on Others Consistent Effort to Exhibit Civil Behavior
	Teamwork skills –Being able to work effectively with anyone with different skill sets, personalities, work styles, or motivation level to achieve a better team result.	Communication Skills, Social IQ Conscious Awareness of Impact on Others Continuous Acknowledgement of Responsibility
	Interpersonal relationship skills –Effectively at building trust, finding common ground, having empathy, and ultimately building good relationships with people at work and in your network.	Social IQ, Communication Skills Conscious Awareness of Impact on Others Continuous Acknowledgement of Responsibility
	Presentation skills –Effectively presenting your work results and ideas formally to an audience that captivates their attention, engage their input, and motivates them to act in accordance to your desired outcome.	Communication Skills Consistent Effort to Exhibit Civil Behavior
	Meeting management skills –Leading a meeting to efficiently and effectively reach productive results. At least 50% of meetings today are a waste of time.	Thinking Skills Consistent Effort to Exhibit Civil Behavior

Figure 3.2

I Have this Skill (Check for Yes)	Self–Regulated Skills Han's Skill Definition	Civility Matrix Element and Link to CEW Definition
	Facilitating skills –Being able to coordinate and solicit well represented opinions and feedback from a group with diverse perspectives to reach a common, best solution.	Organizational Cultural Competence, Communication Skills Consistent Effort to Exhibit Civil Behavior
	Selling skills -Building buy-in to an idea, a decision, an action, a product, or a service. This is not just for people in sales.	Communication Skills, Thinking Skills Consistent Effort to Exhibit Civil Behavior
	Management skills –Creating and motivating a high performing team with people of varied skills, personalities, motivations, and work styles.	Social IQ, Communication Skills, Organizational Cultural Competence Conscious Awareness of Impact on Others Continuous Acknowledgement of Responsibility
	Leadership skills –Defining and communicating vision and ideas that inspires others to follow with commitment and dedication.	Social IQ, Communication Skills, Organizational Cultural Competence Conscious Awareness of Impact on Others Continuous Acknowledgement of Responsibility
	Mentoring/ coaching skills -Providing constructive wisdom, guidance, and/or feedback that can help others further their career development	Social IQ, Communication Skills, Organizational Cultural Competence
		Conscious Awareness of Impact on Others Continuous Acknowledgement of Responsibility

Figure 3.2 (Continued)

Conventional: List of people skills you can find in most job descriptions, and you will be assessed on some or all of these in your performance reviews depending on your level.

People Skills *Tribal*

List of people skills that you will not typically find in job descriptions. They are also essential to your career success. I call it tribal because they are more *insider knowledge* that you gain from work experience or from mentors. Some people can go through their entire career and not be aware of some of these skills.

I Have This Skill (Check for yes)	Self-Regulated Skills Han's Skill Definition		Civility Element and Link to CEW Definition
	Managing upwards –Proactively managing your relationship with your boss, his expectations of your work, and his perception of your performance. Whether you are challenged, given opportunities, or recognized at work heavily depends on your ability to communicate, manage expectations, and build a good relationship with your boss.		Social IQ, Communication Skills, Organizational Cultural Competence Continuous Acknowledgement of Responsibility
	Self-promotion skills –Proactively and subtly promoting your skills and work results to people of power or influence in your organization and network. It is not enough that your boss knows you do great work. You need to subtly build your reputation with all key people that can influence your performance review. This is because hard work alone does not guarantee success.		Social IQ, Communication Skills, Organizational Cultural Competence Conscious Awareness of Impact on Others Consistent Effort to Exhibit Civil Behavior
	Skills in dealing with difficult personalities –Being able to still achieve the work result needed while working with someone whom you find difficult.		Social IQ, Communication Skills Conscious Awareness of Impact on Others
	Skills in dealing with difficult/unexpected situations –Being able to stay calm and still are effective when faced with an unexpected or difficult situation. This includes being able to think on your feet and articulate thoughts in an organized manner even when you are not prepared for the discussion or situation you are in.		Social IQ, Communication Skills, Organizational Cultural Competence, Continuous Learning Conscious Awareness of Impact on Others
	Savvy in handling office politics – Being able to understand and proactively deal with the unspoken nuances of office and people dynamics so you can protect yourself from unfairness as well as further your career. Office politics is a fact of life. If you don't choose to play, it can play you.		Social IQ, Communication Skills, Organizational Cultural Competence, Continuous Learning Conscious Awareness of Impact on Others
	Influence / persuasion skills –Being able to influence perspectives or decision making but still have the people you influence think they made up their own minds.		Communication Skills Conscious Awareness of Impact on Others
	Negotiation skills –Being able to understand the other side's motivations and leverage and reach a win-win resolution that you find favorably, satisfies both sides, and maintains relationships for future interactions.		Social IQ, Communication Skills, Organizational Cultural Competence, Continuous Learning Continuous Acknowledgement of Responsibility

Figure 3.3

What will Civility Look like in 2025?

This information is based on outcomes of Weber Shadwick, Civility in America 2018 Survey[11].

What will Successful Civility Training Look like?
Observations from the field.

Okay, so once you understand that soft skills are an essential part of competency related to people-treatment, and that the skills that underpin the ability to be civil are soft skills, you will presumably include a reference to soft skills in your definition of civility. Having a clear definition will enable you to outline performance indicators specific to your workplace, and this will provide a means for measuring behavior change on the job, that is, the transfer of new knowledge and skills to the workplace. And, once you can see the skills applied to the job, you will have a way to measure the overall impact of the skill gain and subsequent behavior change on the job. Specifically, you should be able to understand if, and how, the training benefited not only the individual, but also the organization. This will show your return on investment.

Three Parts to Devising an Evaluation Strategy

There are at least three parts to devising an evaluation strategy:

1. Outlining performance indicators. Performance indicators will be specific to the organization, to the role of the employee(s) being trained, and to the skill(s) being addressed. As an example of an indicator, let us say we choose a skill statement like "show respect for time." Performance indicators for this skill would include behaviors such as:

   a. Adhere to workplace policy stating that *on time* means ready to work at the designated start time

   b. Use e-mail protocol where up to three issues, questions, or notations are included in one email, rather than one e-mail for each, as a means of saving the reader time

---

[11] Shandwick, W., and T. Powell. 2018. "Civility in America 2018." https://webershandwick.com/wp-content/uploads/2018/06/Civility-in-America-VII-FINAL.pdf.

   c. For example, work *start-time* and *end-time* means 9:00 a.m.–
     5:30 p.m., Monday–Friday

   d. Schedule meetings with a 10-minute closing buffer to enable
     meeting attendees to get to their next meetings on time, for exam-
     ple, do not schedule meetings immediately back to back; 3–4 p.m.
     and then 4–5 p.m.

   e. Reserve social communications for nondesignated work time, for
     example, breaks and lunch hour, as a means of maximizing pro-
     ductivity during designated work time

2. Monitoring transfer of skills: Monitoring transfer of skills means looking for, and tracking, transfer of knowledge and skill gain to the workplace. For each desired behavior that will become part of the workplace
standard, you need to outline specific examples—we call these *indica-*
tors, of what the skill looks like on the job. Using our preceding example *show respect for time*, we would be training people in the *knowledge*
and skill areas they need to use time effectively on the job. This might
include learning a digital clock, arriving 10 minutes before a scheduled
shift, or never being late for meetings. For example, for a skill called
communicate effectively via e-mail, we would include indicators such as
"use e-mail protocol where up to three issues, questions, or notations
are included in one e-mail." This protocol might include instructing
trainees to write subject lines in a specific way, for example, *three issues*
or *response required; three questions*. After the training, we would be
able to monitor if and how frequently trainees are writing subject lines
in this way—relative to how many times they were doing this before
the training. As part of your evaluation strategy, you will need to determine what will be measured, and when, and how, and by whom.

3. Measuring bottom-line impact(s). Again, using *show respect for time*
as an example, we would have identified why this skill is important
in building a culture of civility (time wasting is considered one of
the more disrespectful workplace behaviors) and also would have
identified how not wasting time will benefit the individual (greater
efficiency, potentially less stress) and the employer (increased productivity and time is money, so potentially cost saving). To measure
the impact on the bottom line, we could attach a monetary value
to each e-mail, for example, via survey or feedback from trainees,
we determine that to read and respond to general or typical e-mail

What will Civility Look like Over Next 5 Years.

Expectation	% Who Agree
Civility training will be mandatory	33
Incivility will be considered a form of harassment	32
Employees will feel more empowered to report acts of incivility in the workplace	30
There will be less incidents of sexual harassment in the workplace than there are now	26
Men will be less likely to dine alone with women from work	25
Robots replacing human workers will be more commonplace	25
Coworkers will refrain from asking about the personal lives of others	25
Firings for incivility will be commonplace	23
People will be less likely to post about their jobs online	22
Any physical interaction will be strictly limited to handshaking	22
Job candidates will be screened for civility	22
Men will not want to mentor women or help advance their careers	21
In corporate settings, working from home will be encouraged	21
Coworkers will do their jobs with as little interaction as possible	20
In addition to business results, managers will be evaluated by their level of civility	20
There will be greater representation of minority groups in the workplace	19
There will be dress codes for men and women	19
Workplace social events will not be as much fun	19
Politics will be prohibited from workplace discussion	19
Employers will hire civility coaches for employees	19
Coworkers will be more collaborative	18
Coworkers will feel comfortable saying what they feel	17
Holiday work parties will be held during the day and families/partners/spouses will be invited	17
Employers will encourage employees to talk about their differences	17
Coworkers will not question others' ideas or recommendations	13
There will be more coworker social events	12

Figure 3.4

might take on average one minute. Then, we audit or survey and establish that prior to training employees or trainees were getting on average 150 e-mails a day. At one minute per e-mail, they are spending on average 2.5 hours a day on e-mail. At a wage of say 45 U.S. dollars per hour, this equals a cost of 0.75 cents per e-mail. If we see that as a result of using the new e-mail protocol most employees reduce their overall number of e-mail by even 10 percent, we can calculate a savings of 15 minutes per employee per day at a value of 11.25 U.S. dollars. If you have got 100 employees for example, that can equal an estimated monthly cost savings of just under 23,000.00 U.S. dollars—and that is just the measurable bottom-line impact. It will be harder to measure the decrease in stress levels, but it is possible to devise a strategy to do that too.

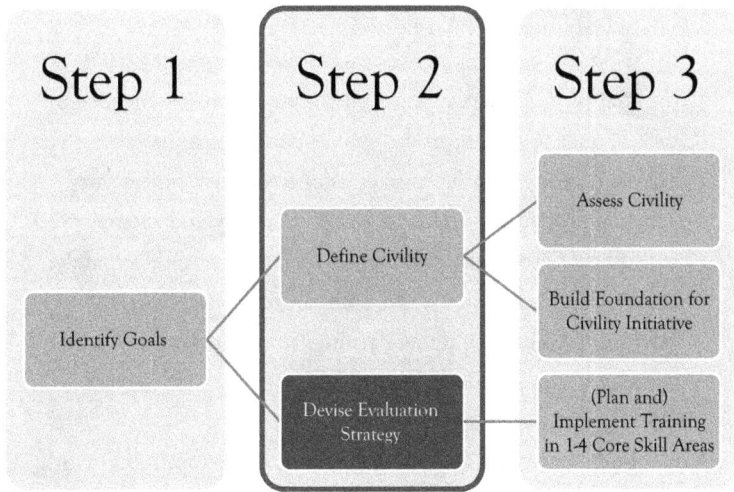

Figure 3.5

What I can tell you for sure is that over the past 20 years, we have worked with many organizations that have experienced at least one, but often several of the measurable bottom-line and other impacts listed at the beginning of Chapter 2 as outcomes of civility training.

Once we know what success will look like, and we know what we plan to measure, we can align these desired and expected outcomes with our training plan.

The Business Case: Impact of Civility Training

Increased Revenue and Engagement

- Companies that openly promote civil communication among employees earn 30 percent more revenue than competitors are four times more likely to have highly engaged employees and are 20 percent more likely to report reduced turnover. Watson Wyatt Civility Survey[12].
- In addition to skills gains, program participants in the UpSkills—Essentials to Excel, (focused on Essential Skills for Hospitality) conducted by the Social Research and

---

[12] "Location Selector." *Willis Towers Watson*, http://towerswatson.com/ (accessed July 3, 2020).

Demonstration Corporation, experienced significant improvements in job performance that were accompanied by a number of positive effects for businesses. A greater breadth of service quality and improved relations with customers were observed, leading to increased customer loyalty, repeat sales, and higher revenues. Increased task efficiency and accuracy led to fewer errors and lower costs of supervision. Ultimately, improved performance was accompanied by greater job retention, leading to higher earnings for employees and lower turnover costs for employers[13].

Increased morale, physical and mental health, and happiness at work:

- According to the American Psychological Association, when employees feel valued by their employer, 92 percent say they are satisfied with their job, 91 percent say they are motivated to do their best, and 89 percent are more likely to report being in good psychological health[14].
- In a civility, respect, and engagement in the workplace (CREW) intervention, there is a six-month process that fosters civil interactions between employees. Participants in the intervention experienced increases in civility with decreases in workplace distress and incivility after completing CREW. These improvements continued to increase one year after the intervention ended[15].

---

[13] David, G. 2015. "New Study Shows Net Benefits of Essential Skills Training in the Workplace." *SRDC*, http://srdc.org/news/new-study-shows-net-benefits-of-essential-skills-training-in-the-workplace.aspx

[14] Psychologically Healthy Workplace Awards 2015, American Psychological Association. 2015. http://apaexcellence.org/assets/general/2015-phwa-oea-magazine.pdf

[15] Michael, P.L. et al. 2012. "Getting Better and Staying Better: Assessing Civility, Incivility, Distress, and Job Attitudes One Year after a Civility Intervention." *Journal of Occupational Health Psychology* 17, no. 4, 425–434, https://doi.org/10.1037/a0029540

Increased performance and productivity:

- The greatest differentiators in performance and achievement are *soft skills* and mindset. Recent scientific studies have established that positive intelligence (PQ) is a significant determinant of how much of your potential for both happiness and professional success you actually achieve. PQ has been directly linked to a wide range of measurable benefits[16]:
  - Sales people sell 37 percent more.
  - Teams perform 31 percent better with high-PQ leaders.
  - Creative output increases three times.
  - People live as much as 10 years longer.
- A study of workplace hiring practices by L'Oreal showed that salespeople hired based on their emotional intelligence made 90,000 U.S. dollars more annually than those hired through traditional methods[17].
- Behaviors involving persistence, self-discipline, effort, and compliance are likely to increase individual worker effectiveness[18].

Increased team orientation and ability to work well with others:

- The high emotionally intelligent (EI) individual, relative to others, is less apt to engage in problem behaviors and avoids self-destructive, negative behaviors such as smoking, excessive drinking, drug abuse, or violent episodes with others. The high EI person is more likely to have possessions of sentimental attachment around the home and to have more positive social

---

[16] "Saboteurs," Positive Intelligence, http://positiveintelligence.com/overview/science/

[17] Joshua F. "The Business Case for Emotional Intelligence." *Academia.edu*, https://academia.edu/1293046/The_Business_Case_for_Emotional_Intelligence

[18] Kunkel, D., and D. Davidson. 2014. "Taking the Good with the Bad: Measuring Civility and Incivility." *Journal of Organizational Culture, Communications and Conflict.* The DreamCatchers Group, LLC. https://questia.com/read/1G1-397579873/taking-the-good-with-the-bad-measuring-civility-and

interactions, particularly if the individual scored highly on emotional management. Such individuals may also be more adept at describing motivational goals, aims, and missions[19].

As discussed in Chapter 2, Defining Civility, once you have gotten your team to agree that a key organizational goal is to build a better workplace, you will plan to implement a civility initiative. Then, you will have to work together to define civility in the context of your organization and understand what it looks like.

Completing these first steps is, in fact, the hardest piece in the civility at work puzzle. But, you have to do it. Without clarifying what civility means in your workplace, it will be very difficult to assess civility, to identify where your training needs are, and to evaluate your success. And, without setting a clear, superordinate, and overriding goal, it will be difficult to know how specifically to empower your teams to choose civility and/or to justify to various stakeholders why their support of this goal is important, and how it will benefit everyone.

Test Yourself

1. According to research carried out by the Carnegie Institute of Technology, what percent of your financial success is because of the skills in *human engineering*?
   a. 85 percent
   b. 45 percent
   c. 22 percent
   d. 91 percent
2. Being able to bounce back after a disappointment or set back, big or small, and continue to move onward and upward is what Lei Han calls:
   a. Tolerance
   b. Stamina
   c. Resilience
   d. Optimism

---

[19] Emotional intelligence http://unh.edu/emotional_intelligence/EI%20Assets/Reprints...EI%20Proper/EI2004MayerSaloveyCarusotarget.pdf

3. *Soft skills* enable individuals to effectively apply technical skills, and exhibiting soft skills requires some technical abilities; soft and technical skills are not necessarily useful independent of each other, this according to:

a. Barker and Knowles

b. Lei Han

c. Dr. Lewena Bayer

d. Steven Covey

CHAPTER 4

Civility at Work: A Change Imperative

….let us use this occasion to expand our moral imaginations, to listen to each other more carefully, to sharpen our instincts for empathy, and remind ourselves of all the ways our hopes and dreams are bound together…

—SU.S. President Obama speech at the memorial
for the Arizona shooting victims

The world is changing. The way people respond to stress and other situations seems different than even five years ago. The way we value each other, and how we act in public, has also changed, and without question, the way we live and work has changed too. And, all this change continues at a rapid rate. Sometimes, the change can be frightening, or difficult, or sad. But, as President Obama suggests in the preceding quote, we need to change our mindset about what we are experiencing. We need to see change as an opportunity to learn. And, this is especially true of changes in the workplace.

An ongoing challenge for businesses today is to manage themselves effectively in times of change, to remain in control when unexpected change arises, and to leverage the positive impact of change. The American Management Association commissioned the Human Resource Institute to conduct a global, in-depth study on strategic agility and resilience. The institute's series of *Major Issues* surveys showed that *managing change* was perennially ranked among the top workforce management issues throughout the 1990s and into this over the past two decades. Some of the main findings were:

- The vast majority of respondents (82 percent) report that the pace of change experienced by their organizations has increased compared with five years ago.

- A majority (69 percent) say that their organizations had experienced disruptive change—that is, severe surprises or unanticipated shocks—over the previous 12 months.
- There are meaningful differences among surveyed organizations in the highest- and lowest-performing categories. Compared with their lower-performing counterparts, higher performers were more likely to:

1. View themselves as agile and resistant
2. See change as an opportunity
3. Say that the pace of change has gotten faster, but remains predictable
4. View themselves as having better change capacities at the individual, team, and organizational levels
5. Engage in strategies such as training to improve managers' change management skills[1]

Additionally, the Conference Board of Canada found that CEOs around the globe identify "speed, flexibility, and adaptability to change" as among their greatest concerns. "Adapt or die" seems to be a prevailing attitude. Accordingly, companies of the future will benefit by finding good ways of measuring their capacity to manage change, that is, their *adaptive capacity*. These organizations will be able to gauge their current agility and resilience and then determine additional needs. When gauging adaptive capacity, organizations will look at four different levels:

- The individual employee
- The team
- The organization
- The industry[2]

---

[1] American Management Association. 2006–2010. "The Quest for Innovation: A Global Study of Innovation Management."

[2] Lotito, M.J. 2012. "Employee Free Choice Act May Increase Economic Uncertainty," SFGate (San Francisco Chronicle, February 11, 2012), https://sfgate.com/opinion/article/Employee-Free-Choice-Act-may-increase-economic-3258674.php

What Does Change Have to Do With Civility?

To survive and thrive in the new world of work, we need to learn continuously, and we need to do so at the pace of change. And, what does this have to do with civility? Well, clearly, implementing a civility initiative in your workplace is going to require change. People, processes, codes of conduct, how you recruit and hire, the way you evaluate performance, and so on. Many of these things are going to change.

One very important aspect workplace civility programs that is not true of all change initiatives is that the process and the work related to civility will necessarily go on for a long, long, time—may be even forever! Remember in Chapter 1 where we talked about how when you approach civility as a change initiative you are never really done?

For some, this realization is going to be an insurmountable barrier to implementing civility as a change initiative. But others, as I was, may instead be inspired to learn more about change and identify ways to overcome barriers to change. Understanding what it takes to achieve positive culture change in workplaces has been a long-term pursuit for me, and it has been key in helping me discover that the best model for building a culture of civility in the workplace is a *change readiness* model—and so the *Civility Culture Compass*® was born. More on this in Chapter 7, but for now, some general discussion on change.

The Stress of Change Can Be Positive

We know from our own experiences that change can be stressful. And, research shows that stress impacts behavior and how we think. Of note:

a. Stress is the number one health threat in the United States[3]

b. 70–90 percent of doctor visits are due to stress-related issue[4]

c. Stress is linked to the six leading causes of death[5]

---

[3] "America's #1 Health Problem." *The American Institute of Stress*, January 4, 2017, http://stress.org/americas-1-health-problem/

[4] "The Effects of Stress on Your Body." WebMD (WebMD, December 10, 2017), http://webmd.com/balance/stress-management/effects-of-stress-on-your-body

[5] Michael, A. 2019. "How Does Stress Affect Us?" *Psych Central*, June 19, 2019, http://psychcentral.com/lib/how-does-stress-affect-us/0001130

While these risks are real, recent research is showing that work strain, when managed correctly, can actually have a positive impact on productivity and performance[6]. When driving change toward a culture of civility, the trick is to change participants' mindsets such that what might be perceived as negative stress becomes good stress, for example, anxiety becomes excitement, fear becomes enthusiasm.

The fact is, stress is unavoidable. "We live in a world of ongoing worry, change, and uncertainty. You have to get used to it," says Justin Menkes, an expert in the field of C-suite talent evaluation and the author of *Better Under Pressure: How Great Leaders Bring Out the Best in Themselves and Others.* "Stress is an inevitable part of work and life, but the effect of stress upon us is far from inevitable," says Shawn Achor, an expert in positive psychology and the founder of Good Think, Inc. Both Achor and Menkes agree that altering your approach to stress can yield positive effects. "Stress can be good or bad depending on how you use it," says Achor. In fact, how you manage pressures can distinguish you as a leader and give you a career advantage.

Positive impacts—stress can:

- Cause the human brain to use more of its capabilities
- Improve memory and intelligence
- Increase productivity
- Speed recovery from things like knee surgery

And, even at high levels, stress can:

- Create greater mental toughness
- Help build deeper relationships
- Heighten awareness
- Foster new perspectives
- Provide a sense of mastery
- Build a greater appreciation for life
- Give people a heightened sense of meaning
- Strengthened priorities

---

[6] Shawn, A. 2014. "Make Stress Work for You." *Harvard Business Review,* July 23, 2014, http://blogs.hbr.org/cs/2011/02/make_stress_work_for_you.html

The findings of Harvard researchers Achor and Menkes (2011) were significant:

A. When an individual thought about stress as enhancing, instead of debilitating, they embraced the reality of their current stress level and used it to their advantage.
B. Positive-minded individuals reported significantly fewer physical symptoms associated with distress (such as headaches, backaches, fatigue).
C. On a scale of 1 to 4, productivity assessment moved from 1.9 to 2.6—a significant shift.
D. Life satisfaction scores also increased, which in previous studies has been found to be one of the greatest predictors of productivity and happiness at work[7].

Change = Learning

As many people have a visceral reaction and assume the worst when they hear the word *change*, we recommend encouraging everyone involved in a workplace civility initiative to replace the word *change* with the word *learning* and to focus on the positive, as well as on the end in mind goals and outcomes, of the initiative. For example:

- Avoid calling your initiative a change initiative, call it a Ready to Learn, or XYZ Workplace Civility Project. Maybe it is an Employee Engagement Program or your Building a Better Workplace Initiative, whatever you like, just try not to put the word change in the title.
- Instead of saying, "As a result of market changes and global trends, we all have to change. We need to work faster and be more agile," say, "We can build on our current skills and take this opportunity to learn as we adapt to trends and market shifts."

---

[7] Shawn, A. 2014. "Make Stress Work for You." *Harvard Business Review*, July 23, 2014, http://blogs.hbr.org/cs/2011/02/make_stress_work_for_you.html

- Do not say, "You need to change how you work," say, "Learning how to work differently will make you more efficient."
- Rather than saying, "You are all required to attend Change Management training," say, "The Continuous Learning course we're all taking, is going to help us manage whatever comes our way."
- Employees are more inclined to get excited about learning opportunities versus requirements to change, and people usually like knowing what the benefit of the change or learning will be, for example, say, "We can all reduce our daily stress by learning how to manage our time better. Attendance requested: Learning opportunity for Supervisors, every Tuesday 9-11am," versus saying, "We are wasting too much time and have to do things differently. Mandatory training for supervisors. Time Management training 6 consecutive Tuesday mornings 9-11am."

When you review Chapter 7, The Civility Competency Matrix, you will learn more about how specific skills such as systems thinking and continuous learning enable you to learn amid constant change. And, you will see how social intelligence and cultural competence skill development can help individual employees and your overall organization be to be both resilient and adaptive, to foster effective communications, and to overcome the challenges that new changes bring. These abilities all support a culture of civility. You may note as you continue on in the chapter how frequently we reference *learning* versus *change*. Think about how doing the same in your conversations about change might shift attitudes about change in your work group.

The New World of Work

While we are talking about change, and before we get too far into planning our civility initiative, it seems prudent to have a look at some trends and influences that may be impacting our workplaces, currently, or in the near future. You will see when we look at the *Civility Culture Compass*® model shortly that these are insights that can help you navigate potentially barriers when starting and managing a workplace civility initiative.

Research and Resources on Trends Impacting the Way we Work

Social Trends

- When and where employees work is changing due to mobile devices: they work at home, during their commute, and on weekends.
- We see an emergence of the 24-hour shift (62 percent work before office commute,
- 37 percent each evening at home, 49 percent in middle of the night if they cannot sleep).
- *Trivialization* of place—employees can work anywhere, anytime, thus much more freedom.
- Many employees have smartphones and tablets and use both for work or personal[8].

How do these social trends impact how we work?

We are not working face to face as much, we are on the go, and we are communicating via technology, so we may lose our ability to read nonverbal and verbal cues. Plus, we may use time differently, and this can be a problem if someone has a different idea of *respect for time*. We may be relying on our devises and not thinking as much.

Employment Issues

- An increase in nonstandard jobs with nontraditional working arrangements
- A decrease in *middle-class* jobs such as middle management with a commensurate increase in *good* jobs (professional, white-collar) and *bad* jobs (unskilled, semiskilled—cashiers, cooks), increases in downsizing and restructuring of organizations

---

[8] 2011, last updated: February 21 Published: September 7, "How Workshifting Is Changing the Way We Work," Small Business Trends, February 21, 2020, https://smallbiztrends.com/2011/09/workshifting-changing-way-we-work.html.

- A definite increase in multitasking and multiskilling (expanding the range of duties and increasing responsibilities) in the modern workplace
- An increase in contract work and part time
- Moving away from job specialists to job generalists
- Management hierarchies generally are flattening
- An increase in automation and artificial intelligence replacing workers[9]

How do these employment trends impact how we work?

These trends can result in stress related to:

- Fewer opportunities for advancement
- Decreased employee loyalty and motivation
- Change fatigue
- Mental and physical health issues, for example, depression, longer periods of unemployment between job changes, longer work terms before retirement resulting in multigenerations at work
- Underemployment due to necessity to take whatever job is available
- Over work and labor shortages
- Job insecurity
- Low morale
- Workforce aging (tension between generations, retirement age, disability concerns), population aging (eldercare pressures for employees), population more ethnically diverse

Also, due to pressures of globalization, the employment relationship is increasingly fragmented, interrelated (networked) and unstable (ongoing mergers and acquisitions)[10].

---

[9] Lee, R., and J. Anderson. 2020. "Experts on the Future of Work, Jobs Training and Skills." Pew Research Center: Internet, Science and Tech (Pew Research Center, May 30, 2020), https://pewresearch.org/internet/2017/05/03/the-future-of-jobs-and-jobs-training/

[10] The Future of Workplace Relations - An Acas View. 2011. "Acas Policy Discussion Papers." https://archive.acas.org.uk/media/2978/The-future-of-workplace-relations---An-Acas-view/pdf/The_Future_of_Workplace_Relations_-_An_Acas_view.pdf.

Technology and How We Do Business

- Mobility, cloud computing, business intelligence, and social media are transforming business: consumer behavior more value-driven, business pace accelerating to *real-time*, and new digital economy (due to technology) creating need for business to become more networked, less hierarchical[11]
- Changes in the structure and composition of information technology (IT): toward cloud computing (more and more will be done with cloud computing including moving analytic data to the cloud and increased application mobility to name a few)[12]
- More flexibility for business in creating IT solutions for use, application, and storage of information[13]
- An increase in the number of employees working at home, 90 percent of companies surveyed plan to invest heavily in productivity-enabling technology such as voice activation and video conferencing, trend toward increasing mobility, and use of smartphones, ongoing blurring between business and personal technology[14]

---

[11] "The New Digital Economy: How It Will Transform Business." by Oxford Economics, Sponsored by PwC, AT&T, Cisco, Citi, and SAP - The Manitoba Chambers of Commerce, Entrepreneurial Spirit – Community Values, https://mbchamber.mb.ca/2011/08/the-new-digital-economy-how-it-will-transform-business-by-oxford-economics-sponsored-by-pwc-att-cisco-citi-and-sap/

[12] Forbes Technology Council Editors. 2020. "Council Post: Watch Out For These 13 Cloud Computing Trends On The Horizon." *Forbes.* Forbes Magazine. https://forbes.com/sites/forbestechcouncil/2020/03/05/watch-out-for-these-13-cloud-computing-trends-on-the-horizon/.

[13] Eric, K. 2018. "What Is Cloud Computing? Everything You Need to Know Now." *InfoWorld* (InfoWorld, October 2, 2018), https://infoworld.com/article/2683784/what-is-cloud-computing.html.

[14] Erica, C. 2020. "Workplace of the Future: How Technology Will Change the Way We Work." *Workplace of the Future: How Technology Will Change the Way We Work - Careers news from Channel Insider* (accessed on July 7, 2020), https://channelinsider.com/c/a/Careers/How-Technology-Will-Change-the-Workplace-of-Tomorrow-333122.

- About 12.1 million workers in the United States are employed
  in the IT industry—with numbers increasing all of the time,
  it is one of the fastest growing markets in the United States[15]
- Effect of social media (defined as "the use of web-based and
  mobile technologies to turn communication into interactive
  dialogue") in workplace has both positive and negative effects
  as it "may simultaneously contribute to productive behaviors
  (task-oriented and relationship-building) as well as unproduc-
  tive behaviors (deviance) at work"[16]
- The Internet is transforming the global marketplace-changing
  consumer behavior and creating new business models[17]
- Industries are transforming because of the application of IT,
  business pace is accelerating—*real-time* business intelligence
  and predictive analysis will be required for faster decision
  making and coping with unexpected market risks and opportunities, and business is reorganizing to embrace the new
  digital economy—toward a network structure and away from
  hierarchy[18]

How do these technology trends impact how we work?

Work has intensified, through application of technology: processes move
swiftly, more tasks are expected, pressure to meet productivity targets
is increasing. And, work is becoming more dependent upon technical
competence, so if you are not tech savvy or digitally competent, this can

---

[15] Mendoza, N.F. 2020. "US Tech Industry Had 12.1 Million Employees in
2019." *TechRepublic* (TechRepublic, April 21, 2020), https://techrepublic.com/
article/us-tech-industry-had-12-1-million-employees-in-2019/

[16] Carlson, J., and Z. Suzanne and H. Ranida and H. Kenneth and C. Dawn. 2016.
"Social Media Use in the Workplace: A Study of Dual Effects." *Journal of Organizational and End User Computing* 28, pp. 1531. 10.4018/JOEUC.2016010102

[17] " The New Digital Economy: How It Will Transform Business" by Oxford
Economics, Sponsored by PwC, AT&T, Cisco, Citi, and SAP - The Manitoba
Chambers of Commerce, Entrepreneurial Spirit – Community Values, accessed
https://mbchamber.mb.ca/2011/08/the-new-digital-economy-how-it-will-trans-
form-business-by-oxford-economics-sponsored-by-pwc-att-cisco-citi-and-sap/

[18] Ibid.

become a very big problem. Technology has enabled all sorts of non-traditional, flexible work arrangements that impact how, when, and if we socialize and how we collaborate. Additionally, working effectively from home requires employees be more autonomous, make decisions, and problem-solve more often without ready access to support, find information, and manage themselves and time in different ways than when operating in a workplace full time. Networking, communication, and the nature of social interaction skills need to be learned and honed for new work at home applications.

Economic Trends

- "The recession and financial crisis that ended in 2009 caused a seismic shift that has reshaped the global business landscape. The world economy is now characterized by sluggish growth in the West, a shift in power to the East, and value-driven customers and rising risks everywhere. At the same time, the downturn has hastened the adoption of key technologies – mobility, cloud computing, business intelligence and social media- that are transforming business and sparking a new wave of wealth creation..."[19]
- There has been an increase in *complex challenges*: globalization, market dynamics or regulation, shortage in qualified talent, increasing competition, proliferation of new technologies, increased customer expectations, mergers and acquisitions[20].
- Globalization, facilitated by technology, has increasingly: allowed fragmentation and outsourcing of production generally; created networked organization (joint partnership

---

[19] "The New Digital Economy: How It Will Transform Business" by Oxford Economics, Sponsored by PwC, AT&T, Cisco, Citi, and SAP - The Manitoba Chambers of Commerce, Entrepreneurial Spirit – Community Values, https://mbchamber.mb.ca/2011/08/the-new-digital-economy-how-it-will-transform-business-by-oxford-economics-sponsored-by-pwc-att-cisco-citi-and-sap/
[20] "10 Trends: A Study of Senior Executives' Views on the Future" by Corey Criswell and Andre Martin for Center for Creative Leadership (CCL) (2007).

arrangements, which increase efficiency and decrease costs, for example, bringing in specialist knowledge and expertise at competitive prices); and facilitated or necessitated ongoing mergers and acquisitions[21].

How do these economic trends impact how we work?
We need to understand how our little piece of the world, our work and so on impact and are impacted by the rest of the world. This requires systems thinking and an ability to connect and collaborate with others as a means of accessing ideas, information, and solutions that might not be immediately accessible from inside our little world. Increasingly, I would say that collaboration is currency, and you have to be a knowledgeable worker to manage the impact of these economic trends.

Demographic Shifts

Canadians are aging, and the birth rate is falling: by 2031, 25 percent of the Canadians will be over 65 (up from 13 percent currently). The Canadian population will rise to 36 million in 2026 and fall thereafter; by 2030, there will be 40 retirees for every 100 working persons. It will be more difficult over next 10 to 20 years to attract immigrants due to competition from other countries, and historical immigrant pools are aging also. After 2030, all Canadian population growth will be from immigration—Canadian immigrants increasingly from Asian and Middle Eastern countries[22].

> While the insights provided reference demographic outlook in Canada specifically, there is little doubt that other countries are experiencing similar demographic shifts.
> *Government efforts directed to keeping older workers in the workforce (including proposed changes to human rights legislation)
> *World population continues to grow overall (U.S. Census Bureau, International Database, and World Population Trends 2011)

---

[21] "The Future of Workplace Relations" by Sarah Podoro for ACAS Policy Discussion Papers (2011).
[22] "Aging Gracefully: Canada's Inevitable Demographic Shift," Bank of Canada, https://bankofcanada.ca/2012/04/aging-gracefully-canadas-inevitable/

How do these demographic trends impact how we work?

Having the ability to work well with others and to understand the impact of cultural and generational issues will be increasingly important. Employers will need to understand how to integrate their organizational culture with the growing number of legal requirements related to accommodation in the workplace. We will all have to build our social skills and communication competencies to overcome gender, generational, cultural, experiential, and communication barriers in the workplace.

Recommended Homework

What leadership looks like in 2030 and beyond?

- Checklist of CEO imperatives in *New Digital Economy* indicates leaders need to be: flexible, forward-thinking, resilient, adaptive, creative, and conversant with social media[23].
- For leadership competency in future, the focus "....should be on key emerging business revolutions: agility (speed in anticipating change), authenticity (must create clarity: articulate a vision, create sense of purpose, build confidence and trust in their teams), talent (develop, engage, motivate), and sustainability (balancing business results with concern for greater good). The winners of tomorrow....will use their skills to remain at the ready, anticipate and harness the power of change, and stay ahead of the shifting business environment"[24].
- "As globalization increases, organizations are continually asked to bridge cultural, geographical and functional boundaries effectively and efficiently"[25].

---

[23] "Game Changers: TMT Leadership Skills Digital Age" in The Digital Theory Media Consulting, http://digitaltheory.ca/pdf/Digital-Leadership-Report.pdf

[24] PriceWaterhouseCoopers. March 2008. "How Leadership Must Change to Meet the Future" p. 23

[25] "Development of Strategic Management and Leadership Skills." Free essays, term papers and book reports, https://essays.pw/essay/development-of-strategic-management-and-leadership-skills-220998

- Leaders need to create emotional resonance with and impact on others[26].
- "Most organizations will not need a 'Lone Ranger' type of leader as much as a leader who can motivate and coordinate a team-based approach"[27].
- Future leaders will need to be conversant with doing business internationally and conceiving strategies on a global basis[28].
- Leaders will need to cultivate resilience in their workforces to navigate change effectively and mitigate effects of employee stress[29].

Additional Influencers

A new pattern of work is emerging as the knowledge economy realizes the potential of new technologies and new organizational models. The changes are occurring in the areas of:

Cognitive competence (increased range of tasks and abilities needed and ability to sort and manage huge amounts of info)

Social and interactive competence (excellence in conflict management and negotiation skills needed due to increased teamwork/collaboration)

Changes in process and place (work becoming mobile)

A new "psychological contract" between employers and employees (expectation of competency development, continuous training, work/life balance[30])

---

[26] Gina, H.B. and R.J. Hughes. 2004. "Leadership Development: Past, Present, and Future." *Human Resource Planning* 27, no. 1.

[27] Ibid.

[28] Ibid.

[29] Vaughan, I. "The Coach Approach in Creating Resilient Teams." SMART HR, https://smart-hr.ca/leadership/the-coach-approach-in-creating-resilient-teams/

[30] Judith H., PhD. 2016. "The Changing Nature of Organizations, Work, and Workplace." *WBDG*, May 10, 2016, https://wbdg.org/resources/changing-nature-organizations-work-and-workplace

Oxford economics: The *New Digital Economy* research paper coproduced by AT&T, Cisco, Citi, PriceWaterhouseCoopers (PwC), and SAP[31] identified six dramatic shifts for which organizations need to prepare:

- The global digital economy comes of age
- Industries undergo a digital transformation
- The digital divide reverses
- The emerging market customer takes center stage
- Business shifts into hyper drive
- Firms reorganize to embrace the digital economy

A great many of these trends and influences were considered in creating the *Civility Culture Compass*®. I encourage you to take some time to consider if and how some of these trends might already be evident in your workplace and/or how they might impact you in the future. Your answers are going to help you identify and predict skills gaps—and this information will be very useful when you are outlining a civility competencies training plan.

The Myth of Change

One very popular business book *Good to Great* by Jim Collins. Collins talks about the *myths of change*. He says, "I want to give you a lobotomy about change. I want you to forget everything you've ever learned about what it takes to create great results. I want you to realize that nearly all operating prescriptions for creating large-scale corporate change are nothing but myths"[32].

Generally, Mr. Collins talks about how in the companies that his team observed making the leap from good to great, "... there was no

---

[31] "The New Digital Economy: How It Will Transform Business" by Oxford Economics, Sponsored by PwC, AT&T, Cisco, Citi, and SAP - The Manitoba Chambers of Commerce, Entrepreneurial Spirit – Community Values,vhttps://mbchamber.mb.ca/2011/08/the-new-digital-economy-how-it-will-transform-business-by-oxford-economics-sponsored-by-pwc-att-cisco-citi-and-sap/
[32] *Good to Great*, Jim Collins, Harper Business 2001.

miracle moment. Instead, a down-to-earth, pragmatic, committed-to-excellence process—a framework—kept each company, its leaders, and its people on track for the long haul." And, this is often how it is with civility as a change initiative. Rarely are there breakthrough moments with civility initiatives. It is through the subtle day-to-day shifts in attitude, through a few extra minutes of paying attention, and through incremental modifications to each individual's way of living in the workplace that civility takes hold. Yes, there is a framework for the initiative to get going, but there is a point where people stop talking and planning, and just do it.

In civility training, we often reference the notion of 212 degrees—how you can be watching the pot of warm water heat up and you know something is happening, but you cannot always see it. There is simmering under the surface, but the water is just warm—not exciting to watch, but you know that if you just keep the pot on the heat, eventually something will happen. And, then, it does. With one small increment, the 1 degree difference from 211 to 212, suddenly the water is boiling. One degree makes all the difference. With one last little effort, you see a big change. Powerful change. You can do a lot with boiling water, cook, sanitize, and so on, and there are beneficial side-effects too. One of the side-effects of boiling water is steam, and you can move a locomotive with steam!

This is how it is with civility in the workplace. You do not always see immediate impact, but things are brewing beneath the surface. People are starting to think differently. They are starting to respond differently, starting to be more attentive. And then, suddenly, there is a boiling point, and all those individual efforts come together to create powerful change. And, there are beneficial side-effects too. In addition to the obvious culture changes such as increased morale, fewer sick days, higher productivity, and others, we may also see employees taking civility home with them, being more polite to their neighbor, social capital increasing in the communities where employees live, and so on.

Collins goes on to list seven commonly held notions about organizational change and explains how they are "wrong, wrong, wrong, wrong, wrong, wrong, totally wrong." His statements are based on research involving over 1,400 companies over five years. In the end, there were five companies that made the leap from good to great, and Collins goes on to explain why. The myths are:

1. The Myth of the Change Program: This approach comes with the launch event, the tag line, and the cascading activities.
2. The Myth of the Burning Platform: This one says that change starts only when there is a crisis that persuades *unmotivated* employees to accept the need for change.
3. The Myth of Stock Options: Stock options, high salaries, and bonuses are incentives that grease the wheels of change.
4. The Myth of Fear-Driven Change: The fear of being left behind, the fear of watching others win, the fear of presiding over monumental failure—all are drivers of change, we are told.
5. The Myth of Acquisitions: You can buy your way to growth, so it figures that you can buy your way to greatness.
6. The Myth of Technology-Driven Change: The breakthrough that you are looking for can be achieved by using technology to leapfrog the competition.
7. The Myth of Revolution: Big change has to be wrenching, extreme, and painful—one big, discontinuous, shattering break.

Myths #1, 2, 4, and 7 can most undermine civility initiative efforts in many workplaces.

Regarding Myth 1, The Myth of a Change Program, I also agree with Collins that you do not necessarily need a *launch* event to initiate the change. With civility initiatives, grand introductions are often actually detrimental to building civility. You need to roll out the plan, sure, but without some immediate evidence of real change taking hold, hype, bandwagon campaigns, politics, and lip service, do not really contribute much to building better workplaces. Often, we see workplaces spending more time and money on the launch than they actually spend on planning and rolling out the initiative. Civility ends up being perceived as the flavor of the month, and employees simply are not buying in anymore.

With regard to Myth 2, The Myth of the Burning Platform: Collins says that many people believe that change starts only when there's a crisis that persuades *unmotivated* employees to accept the need for change.

The fact is, we are in the middle of a civility crisis in most workplaces. Civility is ongoing. It is already happening, and so we are well beyond waiting for an alarm to go off, the bells have been ringing and ringing and ringing. Employees are unmotivated to change *precisely* because they have been in crisis for a long time. I believe most are dumb and numb already. By this, I mean that incivility is well enough ingrained in daily work life that many employees do not even recognize it anymore. They are numb and desensitized. And, where or when they recognize incivility, they remain quiet—dumb, unable, or unwilling to raise the issue; tired of talking about it; or incapable of navigating the often difficult conversations required to address it.

This leads us into Myth #4—the Myth of Fear as a Motivator. Yes, fear is a motivator alright, but not a motivator to be more civil. Remember, people are desperate. Fear in uncivil workplaces tends to drive desperation not motivation. And, many desperate people are very afraid of change. Eliminating workplace stress, being healthy, being treated with respect, autonomy, self-mastery, shared purpose, and so on, when it comes to fostering civility, these are the real motivators, and fear is not!

Lastly, Myth #7, The Myth of Revolution: Big change has to be wrenching, extreme, and painful—one big, discontinuous, shattering break. This is absolutely *not* true of civility initiatives. When done properly, imbedding civility is about implementing a series of subtle process changes, it is about incremental shifts—many of which are actually easy to achieve, do not cost much, and end up being self-directed by engaged individuals who are empowered and encouraged to bring their best selves to work every day.

Collins also references an ancient Greek parable that distinguishes between foxes, who know many small things, and hedgehogs, who know one big thing. He states, "All good-to-great leaders, it turns out, are hedgehogs. They know how to simplify a complex world into a single, organizing idea, the kind of basic principle that unifies, organizes, and guides all decisions. That's not to say hedgehogs are simplistic. Like great thinkers, who take complexities and boil them down into simple, yet profound, ideas. Leaders of good-to-great companies develop a Hedgehog Concept that is simple but that reflects penetrating insight and deep understanding." When I read this excerpt, I was validated. For years and years, I have been trying to explain to clients and others how building a culture of civility is maybe complex in process, but that the overall concept is simple—you want to build a better workplace. Sometimes, they get it, sometimes they do not. But, if you are looking to create change that will increase engagement, performance, and profitability in your workplace, your *hedgehog concept*, the basic principle that will unify, organize, and guide decisions, is not complicated. *Choose civility.* That is it. It is really a very simple concept.

Test Yourself

1. What is the connection between change and civility?
    a. Implementing a civility initiative in your workplace will require change
    b. Change is a process and change initiative of civility is never truly finished
    c. The change initiative of civility in the workplace requires individuals to be *change-ready*
    d. All of the above
2. What is not a positive outcome of stress?
    a. Greater mental toughness
    b. Heightened awareness
    c. Ability to multitask
    d. Strengthened priorities
3. What is a trend that is effecting the way we work and do business?
    a. The weather
    b. Fashion trends
    c. Demographic changes in the workforce
    d. The cost of coffee

CHAPTER 5

The Civility Culture Compass

The hardest decision we have to make is whether we live in a friendly universe or a hostile universe...

—Albert Einstein

We have already established that civility is a values proposition (Chapter 2). It is something that you believe in that becomes a point of character. With consistency of practice, civility becomes who you are, more so than something you do. Civility is what motivates you to do the good and right thing and what helps you determine what the good and right thing is. When applied practically, civility as a core value drives your decision making. It influences how you communicate and directs how you behave. For most of us, learning to be civil is at first an experiential exercise, that is, our attitudes about kindness, and respect, and compassion, and graciousness, and generosity, and so on, that develops as a result of our childhood experiences and upbringing. Influenced by our frame of reference, we develop certain perspectives on respect and related values, about our self-worth and our place in the world, and these attitudes certainly influence how we interact with our families and/or in early relationships at school and socially. It is reasonable to presume that we carry these attitudes forward into our workplaces and communities.

Unfortunately, given the high incidence of incivility in the workplace and the frequency and extent to which most of us are exposed to toxic behavior, it would seem that even those of us who grew up in civil environments are taking on the unruly behavior and negative attitudes that uncivil workplace cultures foster. How is this happening?

What is causing these lovely, polite, respectful people to turn into office bullies?

What is causing our internal civility compass to veer off a path of respectfulness and move toward incivility and negativity?

How can we get back on track?

What Comes First, Uncivil Attitude or Uncivil Behavior?

This is a long-debated question when it comes to civility. What is your opinion? If you read the Introduction, you already know my views on this issue. I believe that for most people, circumstances result in uncivil behavior (and desperation), which result in negative thinking, and then, because we do not experience the positive impact of civility often enough, we end up with uncivil attitudes. These attitudes manifest as thinking patterns and they direct and guide our behavior.

About Attitude

In his book, *The Conditions of Learning*, Robert Gagne, defines attitude as "A mental state that predisposes a learner to choose to behave in a certain way." So, when we devise attitudinal training, the goals typically include asking training participants to choose to do something, or to choose to think something. In the workplace, the choices we want the participants to make would usually relate to some key organizational value proposition. Changing attitudes requires changing a person's experience so that his or her perceptions and opinions change. Then, as a result of these shifts, the individual will choose to adopt a new attitude, and this results in new behavior.

Regardless of which comes first, uncivil behavior or uncivil attitude, many of us navigate through life, or at least our work life, with our internal compass veering off in negative directions because it is our habit to do so and that is the terrain we are familiar with. I like to think of this internal force, akin to the magnet that directs a compass needle, as a person's morality, conscience, and/or values. While it is allowable to be human and to make some mistakes, I believe, as adults, we are responsible for our choices—ultimately, we have the power to choose what we do and how we think, where we go and who we go with, how we act and what we say. We need only decide to set our compass in the right direction and choose civility. Albert Einstein said that "...the hardest decision we'll have to make is whether we live in a friendly universe or a hostile universe..." I believe it is that once you make this decision, the second decision you have to make is whether you will contribute to the universe you choose in a positive or negative way.

Sometimes our *compass* points us in the wrong direction. This does not mean we are bad people. It just means we are making poor choices. And, in some workplace contexts, we are inclined to behave badly more often because the pull toward incivility is very strong.

Why Are People Rude at Work?

In many workplaces, this negative force toward incivility gets stronger because:

a. Choosing incivility is easier than choosing civility—when you are tired and busy and stressed, there is little time or energy left over for thinking about others.

b. In many workplaces, it seems there are more reward than consequences for being uncivil.

c. Some of us have not experienced civility enough to recognize it—we are not learning to be civil through our experiences and interactions at work, and without experiencing civility, it is difficult to understand the benefits of it.

d. The written and unwritten rules have changed so much, and are changing ongoing, so many of us just are not sure of the current expectations, and so, we mirror the behavior of whomever seems to be leading at a specific time, in a specific context.

e. Civility in the workplace has been dismissed for a very long time as something *nice to have*, and so, it is rarely strategically or formally taught. We focus on what we consider to be *need-to-have* skills, which typically do not include *soft* skills like sensing the mood of others, being empathetic, monitoring our emotions, interpreting nonverbal cues, showing appreciation, practicing restraint, and so on.

f. Even when they know what civility is, many people simply do not have the skills they need to exhibit civility in an ever-changing workplace.

Time and time again, the outcomes of workplace civility audits conducted by the Civility Experts Worldwide team reinforce my view that where incivility has become a problem, it is usually *not* because employers and/or employees do not want a civil workplace. And, it is usually *not* because either, or both, the employee group and the employer are not willing to do the work to make their workplace civil. Instead, in most workplaces, disrespectful behavior has simply been adopted as habit. Over time, these bad habits, behaviors, such as *abuse of time and resources*, inappropriate tone of voice, language that fosters negativity, and poor e-communication skills, become the norm in the workplace. These norms are often so well ingrained that changing them seems an impossible endeavor. Further, people have lived with the uncivil behavior so long that they often do not even know what *civil* looks like anymore. They give up, they disengage, and they stop believing that a better workplace is even a reasonable expectation.

Wayne Dyer, a well-known author and motivational speaker, said in reference to love and kindness, "*You can only give away what you have to give.*" Similarly, I believe you have to experience civility in order to be able to extend it to others. Many people do not experience civility often enough to recognize it, so they are unable to extend it to others. They would be willing to think, act, and speak differently, but they do not know what is expected, and so, it is hard to know where to begin to change things.

It is actually quite astonishing how, as an outsider looking into a workplace, you can see all kinds of overtly uncivil behavior that people living in the organization do not even identify as uncivil. The fact that employees would say, for example, that chronic lateness, inappropriate language, poor communication skills, and the like are just something they live with at work so that it does not bother them much anymore explains why even when people are sick more often, or less productive overall, they still do not see the connection between toxic workplace culture and their physical and/or mental conditions. We see too how people can exhibit a toxic behavior out of habit for a long time before even realizing they too are contributing to incivility at work. In fact, accepting incivility is contributing to incivility. If the realization that a particular behavior has changed what used to be a positive attitude into a negative one is not enough to compel a person to change the behavior, or if the individual benefits by being uncivil, we know then that the incivility virus has taken hold. When the workplace conditions actually support incivility, rude behavior becomes a part of the fabric or personality that makes up the organizational culture.

In terms of changing workplace culture, many people assume (as mentioned in Chapter 2, Defining Civility) that behaviors described as uncivil *always* reflect an uncivil attitude. Because it can be extremely difficult to change adults' attitudes, it is also then assumed that there is very little we can actually do about incivility at work. As a result, many organizations put in place strategies such as a respectful workplace policy, which are strictly designed to manage behavior.

In my view, there are two potential problems with this approach. First, exhibiting a particular behavior out of habit does not necessarily reflect a specific attitude. And, in cases where this is true, behavior modification can be an unnecessary and costly approach. Sometimes, awareness raising is enough to bring a positive attitude back to consciousness and change a toxic behavior. Second, in and of itself, I do not find that respectful workplace policies are effective tools for changing uncivil behavior because they often just *talk* about what should or could happen *after* the incivility has occurred. It is as though we are saying, "Accept that incivility is going to happen. You can't stop it, so just learn how to deal with it." It seems to me that through this approach, we are perpetuating a sort of learned helplessness, and in many ways, co-developing a culture of mistrust and disengagement.

If, as per Stephen R. Covey's insight quoted at the beginning of Chapter 7, "you can't TALK yourself out of problems you've BEHAVED yourself into," the problem of incivility can only be resolved by being, thinking, and acting differently—this is so that the incivility does not happen in the first place. One way to do this is by creating workplace environments where incivility cannot survive and certainly cannot thrive.

In a workplace context, where incivility can be attributed to a lack of experiential education, I find that people are usually not behaving civilly because they do not know any better. Or, they have specific attitudes about respect and civility based on what they may *not* have experienced. And so, the plan for fostering a culture of civility in the workplace is to change their experience.

We do this by:

A. Creating an environment where positive change (learning) is required and supported—this is to replace an environment where bad habits and negativity have been endorsed over positive change/learning
B. Encouraging (and in fact requiring by way of policy and procedure) this positive change in the form of behavior in four key skill areas that underpin an ability to be civil

Then, because of the measurable benefits of the new civil behaviors being exhibited consistently and more frequently, we can change peoples' experiences. These positive experiences often result in attitudinal changes, and when we can shift paradigms, we can change organizational culture. We will be getting into this in more detail in Chapter 7, Competencies that Support a Culture of Civility.

The *Civility Culture Compass®* offers a model for a creating a culture of civility in your workplace. The compass outlines a proactive, competency-based approach to shifting organizational culture from toxic and negative to respectful and positive.

If you are following the three-step process for implementing a civility initiative, our discussion here is the first substep in Step 3 (see the following chart).

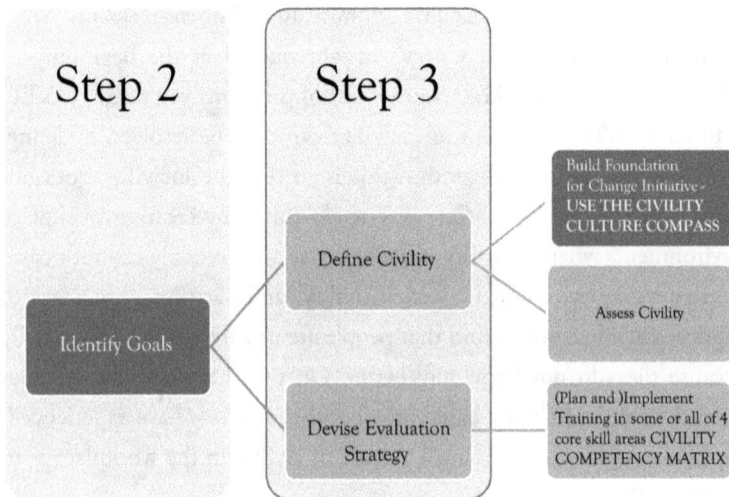

Step 2

Step 3

Identify Goals

Define Civility

Devise Evaluation Strategy

Build Foundation for Change Initiative - USE THE CIVILITY CULTURE COMPASS

Assess Civility

(Plan and)Implement Training in some or all of 4 core skill areas CIVILITY COMPETENCY MATRIX

Figure 5.1

What Is Organizational Culture?

Culture is an anthropological concept. But, in the field of organizations, it refers to the values, beliefs, activities, style of communication and interaction, and rituals that determine an organization's character or *personality*. A company's culture can support or hinder the realization of its own vision and objectives, encourage or stifle collaboration and creativity, make it more difficult or easier to accomplish great things by its people, and so on. The organization's culture has the power to shape people's practices and behavior within it, but fortunately, we also can shape our organizations' culture by our determined understanding of cultural dynamics, and by taking action to mold the culture in a way that reflects our vision and values[1].

As discussed in Chapter 4, it is our understanding that because we are looking to change behavior and attitude to effect organizational culture in a positive way, that imbedding civility in your workplace is a change initiative.

Here is an overview of how this works:

- A civility change initiative is a three-step process (preceding chart) that utilizes the *Civility Culture Compass*® model to build a foundation—that is, create conditions that support a culture of civility.
- Once the foundation is in place—you will have identified, assessed, and addressed:
  - Change—the past, current, and future situation
  - Alignment—the clarity and cohesiveness of your goals and understanding of the same across the leadership team
  - Engagement of work team
  - Readiness—*competency-wise*
- Building on the foundation, you will devise a training plan to build civility competencies. The civility competency training plan is based on the *Civility Competency Matrix*®, which details the skills required in four key areas related to competency in civility.

---

[1] Extracted from HumanNext LLC, www.humannext.com, Cultural Competence Profile.

- In implementing the civility initiative, you will use a range of tools, such as assessments, evaluation strategies, training plans, and you will engage in various activities, including assigning tasks to various stakeholders.

You may be tempted to use some of these tools as standalone solutions, and while they may be useful to some degree independently, it is important to recognize that the tools in and of themselves are not enough to facilitate real, long-lasting change. This recognition comes as a result of our experience with past civility initiatives but also through the experience of others.

As an example,

[…] like time management tools alone won't solve your time management issues, change management tools and techniques are not enough to ensure organizational change success. Leaders must shift their thinking about how change is facilitated in their organizations and integrate an understanding of the change process into all their leadership practices. In an age where there is an 'app' for everything, it is not surprising that leaders often look at organizational change from the perspective of the tools. However, there are three potential risks when you view change from this perspective:

1. You lose sight of the intended outcome, focusing instead on getting the tools or technology implemented.
2. You place the right tool in the wrong hands, thus negating its value to your organization.
3. You compartmentalize the change from the wider context of your organization, thus limiting your ability to increase your organization's capacity for change.

Research has shown compartmentalizing the change and focusing on the tools and techniques instead of the leadership and management of the change is one reason for the high failure rate[2].

---

[2] *Karp, T. and Helgo, T. (2008). From change management to change leadership: embracing chaotic change in public service organizations.* Journal of Organizational Change Management 8(1), 82–96.

Successfully changing uncivil, negative workplace cultures to civil, positive workplaces comes as a result of all the components of the model fitting together in a specific way.

Skills Versus Competencies. What Is the Difference?

Once suitable conditions for implementing a civility initiative have been achieved, the next step will be to devise a training plan to build competency in civility. When individuals across an organization reach a baseline level of competency in civility, the resulting attitudes and behaviors begin to create a culture of civility. For our purposes in this book, we are making an assumption that, barring any psychological or physical barriers, every person has an inherent capacity to be civil.

Civility as a core competency requires that an individual can exhibit certain measurable and related knowledge, skills, abilities, and commitments, and to do so consistently, in a way, and at a standard prescribed for application in a specific context, for example, a workplace, in a way that is deemed effective for that context.

A competency is more than just knowledge and skills. It involves the ability to meet complex demands, by drawing on and mobilizing psychosocial resources (including skills and attitudes) in a particular context[3].

The specific knowledge, skills, abilities, and commitments that a person competent in civility can exhibit are outlined in the Civility Competency Matrix® (see Chapter 7). For our purposes, a *skill* is defined as:

- Behaviors and/or knowledge that are learned through experience, including both technical and soft skills
- Something you exhibit, what you do, or carry out for a specific purpose, for example, to achieve a predetermined result on the job

With the skills related to civility, *how* you use the behavior or knowledge is extremely important, and this awareness is often what identifies degrees of competency related to civility.

---

[3] Debbie Morrison, "Online Learning Insights," Online Learning Insights, February 6, 2017, http://onlinelearninginsights.wordpress.com/

The Civility Culture Compass®

Using the Civility Culture Compass®

The *Civility Culture Compass®* is used to assess four organizational conditions, which when *ideal*, as described next, increase the success of civility initiatives. These conditions are:

- Change
- Alignment
- Engagement
- Readiness

The extent to which you can identify that the *ideal* conditions for each of the four compass settings are met will:

A. Predict how effective a civility change initiative will be if implemented in your organization at the current time
B. Identify where conditions need to be addressed to increase the success and sustainability of your civility initiative

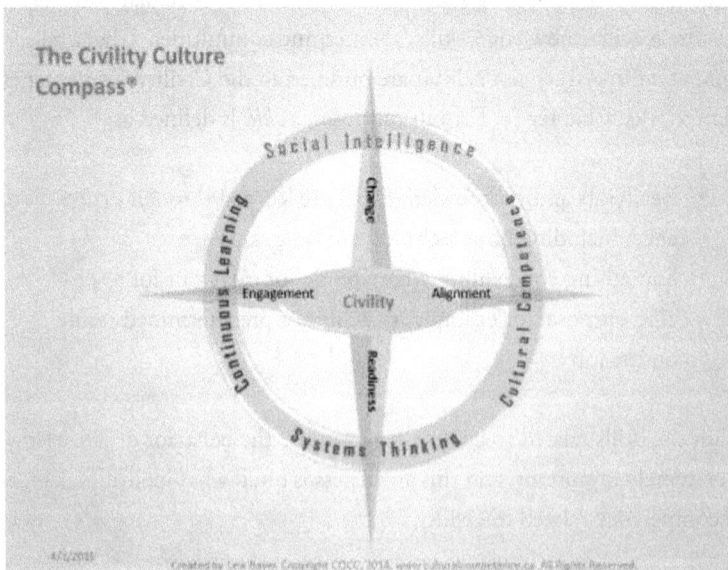

Figure 5.2

C. Help pinpoint contextual and conditional aspects that may contribute to incivility in your workplace

D. Enable your team to plan a cohesive and comprehensive civility initiative

E. Provide a starting point for building skills in four key competency areas that support ability to be civil, for example, by devising a training plan

Four "Conditions" on the Compass

Change—references the current context relative to change. What has happened in the organization in the last 6 to 12 months, what is currently happening or changing, and what changes are anticipated for the near and distant future?

- **Change**—Before implementing a civility initiative, *ask*:
  1. What is the current situation?
  2. Have there been recent changes in the organization?
  3. Are there changes pending?

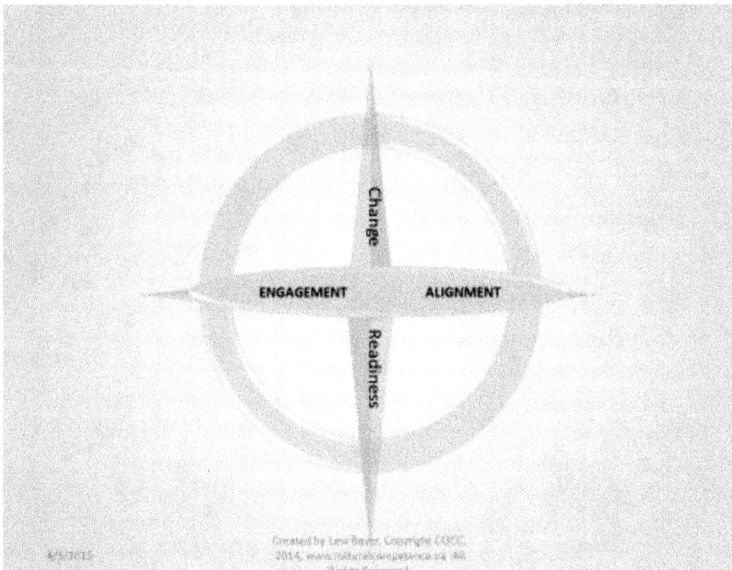

Figure 5.3

4. Any change ongoing?
5. Any changes anticipated in the community, sector, industry, or globally that could be impacting the organization now or in the near future?
6. Do we understand the current need for change? For example, why do we think we need change?
7. How receptive are we to change? For example, are our employees resistant?

We ask these questions as a means of understanding if this is the right time for implementing a civility initiative. We want to know if there will be distractions that we cannot control. Are we anticipating personnel, logistic, or economic changes that could derail or influence our efforts? As an example, if the change-makers spearheading the civility initiative are retiring within 12 months, it is not that we need to completely postpone the initiative, but we may need to consider how we will transition leadership of the initiative 8 to 10 months in. Or, let us say we are in the process of implementing LEAN, maybe we need to consider whether the volume of training required to transition to LEAN might result in our employees being too training-fatigued to take on civility skills training concurrently.

Ideal conditions related to change would be:

- No recent (e.g., in the past 60–90 days) significant changes that employees may still be recovering from
- No significant changes planned (e.g., mergers, downsizing, relocation) planned for 3–6 months
- Employees' overall attitude about change has been assessed; hopefully a receptivity to change has been identified
- Awareness of untenable status quo

Enabling factors: Clear goals, full communication of background and rationale for change

Hindering factors: Lack of engagement, fear, low trust, unclear goals, uncertainty, unclear rationale

Skills that support a condition of change: Continuous learning, thinking skills: specifically systems thinking and problem-solving ability. Employees need to be able to adapt to change, to be resilient, and to seek to understand context and consequences ongoing—these are outcomes of continuous learning ability.

Alignment—references the extent to which the organizations policies, procedures, values, mission, and so on are currently aligned with, or positioned to support, a culture of civility.

- *Alignment*—Before implementing a civility initiative, *ask*:
    1. Do our organizational values include civility? If not, why not?
    2. To what extent are day-to-day activities, behaviors, policies, and processes currently aligned with the overriding goal, which in the case of most civility initiatives relates to building a better workplace?
    3. Is anything we are currently doing contrary to a culture of civility? (This is where we highly recommend even a short consult with a civility expert who may be able to pinpoint activities, policies, behaviors, and even processes that you do not immediately recognize as contributing to incivility in the workplace.) As examples:
- Are we telling people we want them to behave civilly, but then actually rewarding and/or encouraging uncivil behavior, for example, is it our practice to holding off starting meetings until the managers or employees who are consistently late arrive, thus rewarding them and essentially punishing those who were on time?
- Do we tell employees that we support and encourage diversity, but then post notices that employees may not speak, write, or even sing in their first languages on the job?
- Do we expect employees to stay overtime or change shift times when we need them, for example, due to unexpected production schedule changes, but at the same time do not expect to occasionally accommodate those employees arriving

or leaving early due to unexpected changes in their personal schedules?

- Do we tell employees that we want collaboration and team-work, but then create an environment where we pit them against each other and require them to compete for attention, accolades, assignments or rewards?
- Do we ask employees to be respectful of company property and safety regulations, but then not follow through on our responsibility to keep those same employees safe at work?
- Do we expect frontline employees to adhere to respectful workplace policy, for example,, disallow profanity on the job, but then also expect employees to tolerate inappropriate language from their managers?
- And, so on....

Ideal conditions related to alignment would be:

- Agreement, and buy-in by leadership, that it is time for posi-tive change (even if they do not know yet what that will look like), for example, this relates to leadership having determined a goal such as Jim Collins' (author *Good to Great*) *hedgehog principle*.
- Managers and leaders have knowledge of desired goals and objectives of the initiative.
- Review (and update if necessary) of organizational values and their definitions.
- Review of workplace policies and procedures and identifi-cation of what is and what is not working from a leadership point of view.
- Willingness and ability to update policies and procedures as may be required.
- Awareness, (general) by leadership, of general human rights, labor laws, bullying legislation, accommodation, and so on.
- Respectful workplace policy in place.
- Aligning the organization to the external environment requires forethought and taking proactive actions. Aligning

employees' performance to the strategic direction requires leadership and monitoring. The strategic plan must be created against the backdrop of the organization's values; its moral compass. These values need to lay the foundation for the accepted behaviors in the organization[4].

- Communication plan in place, for example, to help communicate company vision and goals to all employees.
- Polling of employees to identify characteristics and/or issues of the current workplace culture from their perspective, for example, ask them via survey or online poll, "What are the three things you would change about your workplace culture?" Or, "What are the top three stressors in your job?" Or, "What policies, behaviors, or activities in the workplace, if not changed or corrected, could potentially lead to you quitting your job?"
- Review and tracking (you can use this data as a starting point for evaluating impact of training down the road) of any or all of the following:
  - Requests for stress leave and/or interoffice transfers
  - Retention rates
  - Sick days
  - Participation in workplace events identified as optional or social
  - Harassment or bullying claims

Enabling factors: Sufficient systems and processes in place to support initiative, direct activities (by setting and rationalizing priorities)

Hindering factors: Poor or unclear communication, ineffective communication system.

Skills that support a condition of alignment: Strategic thinking and systems thinking—specifically, employees need to be able to take on a big picture

---

[4] Nu-Leaf Nursery, "Strategic Thinking - A Task for All Employees," PRLog, https://prlog.org/10434384-strategic-thinking-task-for-all-employees.html.

perspective on problems, situations, and events. They need to view information from different perspectives and points of view, to interpret implications and make appropriate recommendations. Social intelligence and cultural competence for leadership—they need to be able to understand employees' perspective, read verbal and nonverbal cues, and assess contextual elements appropriately.

Some suggestions for additional alignment assessments are included in Chapter 9, Tools You Can Use.

Engagement—When we talk about engagement, we are talking about how consistently, and to what extent, employees are choosing to contribute to the organization in a meaningful way (beyond the basic requirements of their job descriptions). By this definition, attendance is not necessarily an indication of engagement. Simply doing one's job at the minimum standard required is participation, but participation does not necessitate engagement. Engagement requires *buy-in*. Engaged employees believe that the work they do, and that they as individuals, have value. Fully engaged employees choose to self-motivate, to be accountable, to work well with others, to find solutions and to be positive. Engagement requires trust—this is key. We will discuss this more in Chapter 6, Assessing Civility. Basically, if engagement is low, the likelihood that employees are ready for change is also low, and the effectiveness of any change initiative—no matter how effective the individual tools are, will be significantly reduced.

Engagement—Before implementing a civility initiative, *ask*:

- To what extent do employees *choose* to participate in non-required workplace activities, for example, social events, team sports, volunteer opportunities?
- Do employees trust us? And, do we trust them?
- Do employees show confidence in our decision making? Or, is there frequent push back and resistance?
- Do employees seem happy at work?
- If we could not offer wage increases, how many employees would stay with us, for example, weather the storm and be loyal?

- When provided with opportunities for growth and training, do employees invest, for example, give their own time or pay part of the cost?
- To what extent do employees support each other, for example, be accountable to each other, have each other's back and/or engage personally/socially as well as at work?
- Overall, how would we rate collaboration in our workplace?
- Have we seen increases in sick days? Turnover? Grievances?
- How do our employees respond to change? For example, are they resilient? Adaptive? Resistant?

Ideal conditions related to engagement in the workplace:

- High engagement, for example, as indicated by high trust, and/or high *happy at work* scores. Engagement should be high:
  - At the leadership level—this is important
  - At all other levels

Enabling factors: Safety (physical and mental), trust across work teams, effective communication, appropriate rewards and incentives

Hindering factors: Fearfulness about job security, tyrannical management style, lack of training opportunities, low or few opportunities for questioning, and open communication

Skills that support a condition of engagement: Continuous learning as it builds self-efficacy and confidence. Systems thinking, which supports adaptive capacity and problem-solving. Cultural competence and social intelligence, which both support empathy, team orientation, and shared perspective among and across work teams.

Readiness—There are two types of *readiness*:

Type 1: Organizational *readiness*—Here we are talking about a readiness and ability for an organization to expend resources such as managements' and/or employees' time and a budget for training. The extent to which we are *ready* resource-wise will determine the timing, scope, and approach of the civility initiative. Additionally, the organization has to actively create a performance and culture management focus that leaders identify, understand, and agree upon during a time of strategic change[5].

Engagement—Before implementing a civility initiative, *ask*:

- Are we prepared to commit our time, money, and energy to this initiative?
- Do all stakeholders understand that this is an ongoing and long-term investment?
- What specifically do we want to achieve?

Ideal conditions for organizational readiness:

- Availability of resources, for example, personnel, time, budget for an initiative
- Identification of a specific goal related to civility, for example, improve retention, eliminate bullying, improve innovation by embracing diversity, reduce stress by increasing respectful interactions
- Existence of plans and structures in place to support the new goals and outcomes—to trace path between mandate—engagement efforts—goals/outcomes
- All employees see the connection between the work they do every day to the company mission or strategic focus regarding the initiative
- Employees' individual goals and work performance measures are connected to the organization's vision re; the initiative

Type 2: Skills readiness—Related to how competent employees (and/or leaders) are in the four key civility skill areas. We are going to employ a range of assessment approaches and methodologies to determine this

---

[5] Flora Richards-Gustafson, "Approaches to Organizational Strategic Alignment," Small Business—Chron.com (Chron.com, October 26, 2016), http://smallbusiness.chron.com/approaches-organizational-strategic-alignment-14151.html.

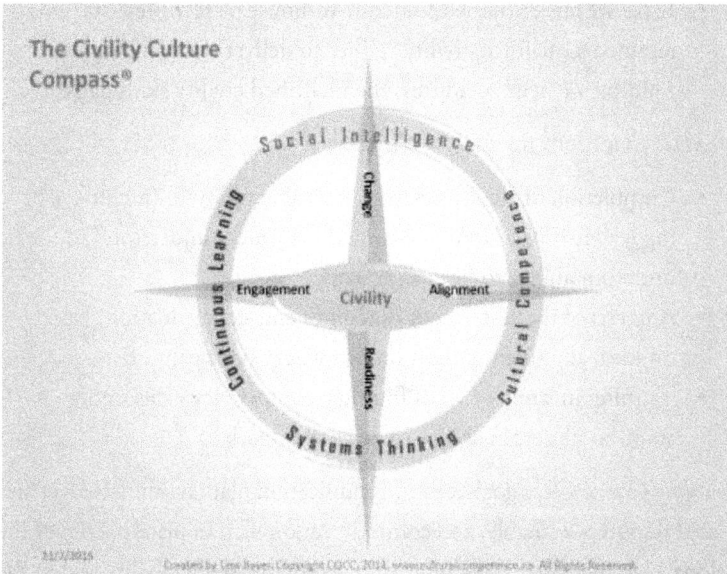

Figure 5.4

readiness. And, the level of readiness will inform our training goals and individual learning plans. The four key skill areas are:

- Social intelligence
- Cultural competence
- Continuous learning
- Systems thinking

Note: These four key skill areas make are outlined on the Civility Culture Compass®.

Ask:

- Have we identified where our leaders and teams are *competency-wise* in the four key competency areas that support the ability to be civil and build a culture of civility at work?
  - Social intelligence
  - Cultural competence
  - Continuous learning
  - Systems thinking

- Have we either trained someone in-house or recruited or retained a qualified civility trainer to deliver the competency training we need to address the identified civility skills gaps?

Ideal conditions for skills readiness:

- Completion of skills assessments by all employees (including leadership) in four key competency areas understood to underpin ability to be civil at work
- Analysis of the assessment outcomes and determination, based on ideal alignment conditions, of where skills gaps exist
- Training in some or all of four key competency areas understood to underpin ability to be civil at work

Enabling factors: Clear goals and communication plan, training budget and related resources available, and communication plan in place to convey the rationale and benefits of training. Trainers well versed in civility and in the loop with respect to the organizations goals and evaluation strategy.

Hindering factors: Training for the sake of training, incomplete or inaccurate analysis of assessments, training fatigue, training only part of the team, training in only one or some of the competency areas but not all, fear.

Skills that support a condition of readiness: Continuous learning in that individuals can self-direct some of the learning. Social intelligence as a means of ensuring communication of the plan and the training approach is appropriate, and systems thinking as a way of devising training plans that support the overriding goals and also support collaboration.

Homework

Civility Culture Compass® General Assessment

For each of the questions listed, ask yourself, AM I...

Ability to be Socially Intelligent

3 Questions

1. Able to perceive others' messages and interpret appropriately given social context?
2. Able to adjust communication or social style in light of others' cultural and personal styles and social context?

3. Knowledge of and ability to recognize what behaviors—written and unwritten—are expected and understood in certain cultures, and in workplace generally?

Ability to exhibit Cultural Competence

3 Questions

1. Show sensitivity to others by striving to understand their perspective and value and respect differences?
2. Are self-directed and appropriate in situations where personal or moral judgment required?
3. Are sensitive to and able to reflect on his/her own cultural heritage, values, and biases, and how they may affect others?

Ability to engage in Continuous Learning

3 Questions

1. Seek chances to acquire knowledge and skills to improve work performance?
2. Willingness to incorporate new concepts, methods, or modalities in learning?
3. Open to learning about other cultural groups and strategies to communicate across cultural barriers?

Ability to Employ Systems Thinking

3 Questions

1. Able to operate effectively within and across systems within the organization?
2. Able to recognize and adapt to needs of interconnected systems?
3. Understand and accept personal role in the context of various systems?

Change

3 Questions

1. Is the organization experiencing cultural change (either influx of individuals from different countries, nationalities, and/or cultures, or change in organizational focus or growth to international markets

resulting in cross-border or cross cultural business relationships, or change in organizational marketing focus to include immigrant population as target customers)?

2. Have the goals and background and rationale related to the change been fully communicated so all employees at every level have knowledge of them?

3. Is there a feeling of receptivity to or agreement with the need for organizational change?

Alignment

3 Questions

1. Is there an effective communication plan in place to relay all relevant information related to the change?

2. Have the *goals* and desired outcomes related to the initiative been fully communicated so that all employees at every level have knowledge of them?

3. Are there structures *and* incentives in place to support goals and outcomes?

4. Do all employees of your organization see the connection of the work they do every day to the company mission or strategic focus regarding the initiative?

Readiness

3 Questions

1. Do you think it is true in your company that people would be willing to make the effort and accept the risks involved in doing something new if: they were sufficiently dissatisfied with the status quo and if information about a proposed change was communicated thoroughly?

2. Do people in your company resist change even if there is a clear vision and objectives, and the change could have a good result?

3. Do individuals and teams within your organization collaborate (work together toward a specific common goal) very well?

Engagement

3 Questions

1. Is there high absenteeism, turnover, negativity, lack of motivation at your company, either generally or within a specific department?
2. Do your departments share or model the vision and values that have been established for your organization?
3. Do company meetings include an open forum, where employees are free to, and feel safe to, openly share ideas, thoughts, questions, and concerns, and are encouraged to contribute to organizational processes?

Test Yourself

1. What are the four key civility skill areas?
   a. Social intelligence, cultural competence, continuous learning, systems thinking
   b. Social intelligence, cultural competence, continuous learning, respectful workplace policies
   c. Social intelligence, cultural competence, systems thinking, kindness
   d. Social intelligence, continuous learning, systems thinking, acknowledging mistakes
2. Which is *not* an element of the civility compass?
   a. Change
   b. Acceptance
   c. Alignment
   d. Readiness
3. How can we foster an environment of civility in a workplace?
   a. Creating an environment where positive change is required and supported
   b. Creating respectful workplace policies
   c. Encouraging (and requiring) positive behavior change in the four skills areas that underpin the ability to be civil
   d. Both a and c
   e. All of the above

CHAPTER 6

Assessing Civility in your Workplace

Learning without thought is labour lost. Thought without learning is intellectual death.

—Confucius

If you are following the three-step process for starting a civility initiative, you will have already set an *end in mind* goal (likely related to building a better workplace). Identifying this goal would have required completing some type of general organizational assessment, for example, based on the four conditions outlined in the *Civility Culture Compass*®. (See Chapter 8 for a sample.)

Hopefully, you have also defined civility, including detailing indicators of what civility looks like in the context of your workplace (these indicators will be used to measure success), so the next step will be to assess civility in your workplace.

What Is a Needs Assessment?

A needs assessment is a systematic exploration of the way things are and the way they should be. These *things* are usually associated with organizational and/or individual performance[1].

The purpose of conducting a needs assessment is to better understand the reason why things are the way they are—rather than the way they should be and how we want them to be. Analyzing the issues and factors that are creating the current situation helps us know what the solution is to get us where we want to be, and where, when, and how we will apply that solution.

---

[1] http://alumnus.caltech.edu/~rouda/T1_HRD.html

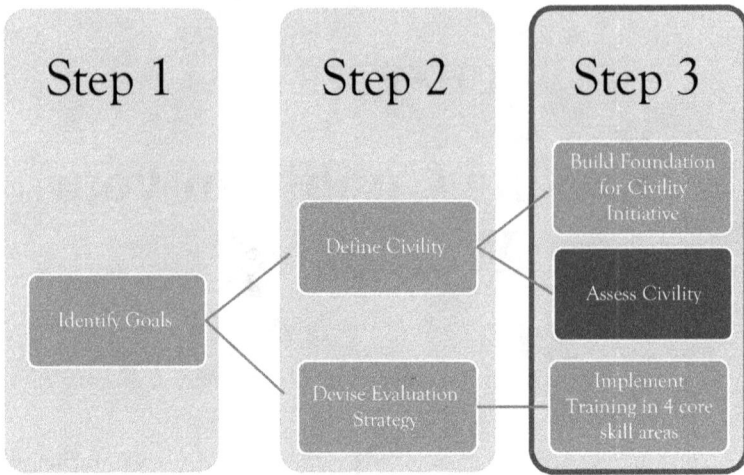

Figure 6.1

We often make assumptions about the reason for things being how they are, and this can result in costly mistakes. For example, if we automatically assume that low productivity in a manufacturing context is due to lack of employee competence, we might spend a lot of time and money delivering training, only to discover that the problem was not competence at all. Maybe the problem was, in fact, outdated equipment or internal systems. Given the speed of change and the cost of these mistakes, organizations simply cannot afford to make rash decisions—needs assessment is an effective way to control some of the investment costs of change.

Another key reason we recommend doing an assessment is that if you use the compass and assess the four civility culture conditions, you may, in fact, find that addressing these conditions solves your problem, and you do not need training after all.

Assessment for workplace training may include assessing one or all of the organization (in its entirely or one or more departments, or divisions), the team(s), or the individual(s).

Some Interesting Statistics About Training

One in three workers thinks the time he or she spent in his or her last training session probably would have been better spent elsewhere, according to a survey by Hudson, a staffing and consulting services company.

Among these workers, 12 percent think the training was a complete waste of their time.

Self-improvement was the main reason for participation in training; 68 percent of the respondents said they attended training because they thought it would provide useful, job-related information. Another 28 percent said they were told to go. The last 3 percent went to training to meet people or to get out of the office[2].

Trainingindustry.com estimates that:

- Average training expenditures for large companies decreased from $19.7 million in 2018 to $17.7 million in 2019. The number for midsize companies dipped $400,000 to $1.7 million in 2019. Small companies barely increased from $355,731 to $367,490.
- Approximately 75 percent of the global spend for training is in N.A. and Europe. Asia and India, the two most populated regions in the world, combined make up about 17 percent of the global market.

Companies spend about 44 percent of their training related dollars on employees, compared to 49 percent on customers, and 7 percent on suppliers and channel partners. Training is an important part of efforts to reduce workplace injury, illness, and death. In the United States, the total cost of workplace health and training alone is over 100 billion U.S. dollars per year[3].

So, after reviewing the preceding statistics, here are some important questions to think about:

1. Would your organization benefit by spending less on training that one in three workers will likely perceive as a waste of time?

---

[2] Katherine Walsh, "Time in Training Often Wasted," CIO (CIO, March 15, 2006), http://www.cio.com/article/2447352/training/time-in-training-often-wasted.html.
[3] "The Effectiveness of Workplace Training," Centers for Disease Control and Prevention (Centers for Disease Control and Prevention), http://blogs.cdc.gov/niosh-science-blog/2010/01/29/training/

2. If planning strategic training in just one to four key competency areas could potentially increase your profitability by 30 percent, would you not want to do that training?

3. If you knew that 67 percent of employees would actively engage in the training indicated in #2, would you not be further inclined to do that training?

4. If you knew you could save time and money by administering one or more quick assessments to identify exactly which of four key competency areas your team needed training in—with little expenditure of time and resources, would you conduct these assessments?

5. If there was evidence that training in one or more of these four key areas could resolve issues related to retention, engagement, and profitability, would you want to engage in this training?

If you answered yes to one or more of the preceding questions, civility training offers a solution to better managing the costs, time requirements, and employee buy-in aspects of workplace training. The next step is completing a needs assessment to identify your training needs.

Benefits of Completing a Needs Assessment

One of the key reasons a needs assessment is completed prior to launching a training plan is to manage resources. Training takes time and money, and so, it just makes sense to have an idea what you are training, why you are training, and who needs the training *before* you train.

There are many additional benefits to completing a needs assessment; these include increased ability to:

- Focus the training on what is important at a specific time for a specific learner
- Identify strengths and weaknesses of learners
- Identify continuous improvements to current structure
- Fit learning to learner
- Identify a future learning path
- Fit trainer to the need of the leaner

- Identify metrics by which to measure success
- Align gaps in goals
- Build a framework for a training communication plan
- Establish expectations for return on investment
- Asses engagement
- Identify risks
- Build a frame of reference
- Enable priorities for action to be established
- Plan the most effective development of limited resources, for instance, to ensure cost effectiveness and value for money
- Justify investment in training by showing how it will contribute to achieving corporate objectives
- Provide a basis for integrating training into the business by getting line management involvement and commitment

Approach to Workplace Civility Assessment

There are two typical approaches to completing a workplace civility assessment:

1. Help people identify performance issues and consider what skills gaps are causing the issues as well as how planned training can help to solve them.
2. Taking a big picture view of the whole organization. Consider current, present, and future activities and goals, and then develop training plans to meet the identified current and anticipated training needs.

Depending on the outcomes you are looking for, you will choose either #1 or #2. For example, if your primary issue is attrition and your goal is retention, you might consider starting with #2. If your issue is a specific employee or group of employees who are not working well together, you might start with #1.

With civility initiatives, because we can often identify elements of overall workplace culture as causing incivility at work, we typically recommend starting with an organizational culture assessment. Primarily, we are assessing the current situation relative to the four conditions identified as strong influences of successful civility training. These are outlined in the Civility Culture Compass®:

- Change
- Alignment
- Readiness
- Engagement

At Civility Experts Worldwide, we customize these civility condition assessments, and much of this process is proprietary. However, there are some general assessments (mostly paper-based) you can use to get started. Details about the sample assessments listed as follows are included in Chapter 11, Tools You Can Use. There is also additional detail in Chapter 10, Sources and Resources. It is always recommended that you use a combination of several needs assessment methods, including:

- Direct observation
- Questionnaires
- Consultation with persons in key positions and/or with specific knowledge
- Review of relevant literature
- Interviews
- Focus groups
- Tests
- Records and report studies
- Work samples

Recommended Assessment Process

While it is understood that identifying a key issue or problem (or more than one) that the organization is looking to address with a civility solution is, in fact, part of assessment, we consider it to be more of an awareness raising exercise for the organization. However, the data collected in completing this prework is used to inform the next steps, which we consider to be the *formal* assessment.

Assessment Process Phase 1: Complete a general organizational culture assessment—Start by asking the questions outlined for each of the four conditions of the compass, as outlined in Chapter 5. And then, if you do not have enough information to move forward, do additional organizational culture assessment.

Sample General Workplace Culture Assessments

- Civility Culture Compass® General Assessment [4]
- The Denison Organizational Culture Survey[5]
- Organizational Health Index[6]
- Organizational Culture Assessment Instrument[7]

Assessment Process Phase 2: After you are able to establish how ideal the current situation is for each of the four conditions, try to identify aspects of any less than ideal conditions that you can adjust. This is achieved through administering additional, targeted assessments—specific to one or more of those four conditions: readiness, change, alignment, and engagement.

Alignment

Some strong indicators of potential misalignment between current organizational processes, workplace culture, and so on, a culture of civility, include: team conflict, quantity of miscommunications, bullying claims, low morale, low retention, and accountability issues.

---

[4] Civility Experts Worldwide - Winnipeg Manitoba Canada, June 25, 2020, https://civilityexperts.com/

[5] Denison Consulting, "Organizational Culture in the Gig Economy," Denison Consulting (Denison Consulting, February 16, 2017), https://denisonconsulting.com/organizational-culture-in-the-gig-economy/

[6] "Solutions," McKinsey and Company, http://www.mckinseysolutions.com/

[7] "Organizational Culture Assessment Instrument Online," Home | OCAI online, http://ocai-online.com/

Sample Alignment Assessments

- Organizational Values Assessment Tool[8]
- Civility Symptoms Survey® Civility Experts Worldwide[9]
- Clark and Landrum Civility Scale® Cindy Clark/Eric Landrum Boise State University[10]
- Ranson Civility Quotient[11]
- Civility Norms Questionnaire[12]
- Positive Culture Assessment[13]

Please see additional information in Chapter 9, Tools You Can Use.

Engagement

There are many indicators of low engagement. Sometimes, it is true that attendance and number of sick days or stress-leave requests seem like obvious signs that people are not engaged. But, these are not always accurate, for example, there may be legitimate physical or psychological reasons a person is not coming to work. Because we understand engagement to mean employees are actively choosing to contribute in a positive way beyond their basic job requirements, we find a stronger indicator of engagement is the overall level of trust. This is because high levels of trust typically correlate with employees stating that:

- They feel valued as individuals
- They feel their contribution has value

---

[8] http://careleaders.com/assessment/valuesAssessment.html

[9] "Assessments: Civility in the Workplace," Civility Experts Worldwide - Winnipeg Manitoba Canada, February 24, 2019, https://www.civilityexperts.com/training-solutions/assessments-civility-in-the-workplace/.

[10] College of Health Sciences, "College of Health Sciences," College of Health Sciences, June 11, 2020, http://hs.boisestate.edu/civilitymatters/research-instr.htm.

[11] "Home - Stop Bullying Tool," Kit, http://stopbullyingtoolkit.org/Civility-Quotient-Assessment.pdf.

[12] Ibid.

[13] "Surveys," Iedex, February 13, 2017, https://iedex.com.au/products/surveys/

- They feel empowered
- They feel that they are treated fairly
- They feel they are compensated fairly
- They feel empowered to self-direct and/or make decisions
- They have a sense of shared purpose
- They feel they can overcome workplace challenges
- They feel supported
- They are happy at work

When the preceding are perceived, people are more likely to perform well and to exhibit positive, respectful behaviors.

Sample Engagement Assessments

- Happiness at Work Survey[14]
- Franklin Covey Trust Quotient[15]
- Organizational Trust and Engagement Index[16]
- Gallup Q12 Engagement Survey[17]

Change

One strong indicator of that change in a workplace that could be inhibiting respectful behavior is the degree of hardiness—hardiness references the physical and/or "bounce-back" from stress and change. Hardiness fosters resilience and resilience of individuals collectively contributes to an organization's overall adaptive capacity.

---

[14] Happiness at Work Survey, accessed July 5, 2020, https://app.fridaypulse.com/help-center/getting-started.

[15] "Trust Quotient Assessment: Trusted Advisor," Trusted Advisor Associates - Training, Workshops, Trust Education, September 28, 2011, https://trustedadvisor.com/our-services/trust-analysis-and-measurement/trust-quotient-assessment.

[16] "Speed of Trust Measurement Tools," The Speed of Trust, https://www.speedoftrust.com/speed-of-trust-measurement-tools.

[17] "Gallup Employee Engagement Center," Gallup Q12 Employee Engagement Center, https://q12.gallup.com/public/en-us/Features.

Sample Change Assessments

- Change Management Readiness Assessment[18]
- Organizational Capacity Assessment Tool[19]
- Resilience Assessment[20]
- Change Resistance Assessment[21]

Readiness

One strong indicator of readiness is understanding whether learners (employees) are physiologically hardy and whether they feel psychologically safe. When employees do not feel their basic needs are being met, it is not likely they will actively participate in learning, and/or the learning will not transfer to the workplace. As an example, if an employee does not feel safe at work, or if he or she feels underpaid or taken for granted, if he or she is unhealthy because of overwork or lack of breaks, he or she may be consciously or subconsciously focused on figuring out how to get these basic needs met. And, if this basic need is not met, learning—no matter how good training is, will not be a priority. (Please see Maslow's Hierarchy of Needs Chart and assessment in Chapter 9, Tools You Can Use.)

---

[18] Tim Creasey, "When Should You Use a Change Management Readiness Assessment?," Prosci, http://change-management.com/tutorial-change-management-assessments.htm.

[19] http://peecworks.org/peec/peec_inst/01795CC4-001D0211.52/M.percent-20Casey percent20Org.percent20Capacity percent20Assessment percent20Tool percent20 percent28paper percent20version percent29.pdf.

[20] "Resilience Assessment," Resilience Alliance - Resilience Assessment, https://www.resalliance.org/resilience-assessment.

[21] Change Resistance Scale, "Conner Partners," 2011. http://connerpartners.com/wp-content/uploads/2012/05/Change-Resistance-Scale.pdf.

Sample Readiness Assessments

- Hierarchy of Needs Self-Test[22]
- Hardiness Test[23]
- Workplace Stress Assessment[24]
- Learning Culture Assessment[25]

Using Assessment Outcomes

Once we have the outcomes of our assessment, we are going to set a training plan goal and outline some learning objectives. We use a version of SMARTER approach to this goal-setting, specifically we consider:

S—specific; what *exactly* do you want to be different after the training?

M—measurable; how will you know there has been behavior change? What will you compare the *after* to?

A—applicable; are you sure these are skills the employees needs to exhibit on the job? For example, do not train just for the sake of training.

R—realistic; can we really teach or train what we need to with the resources available?

T—teachable; are we sure, for example, via assessment, that the identified gaps are based on *skill versus will*? For example, not so easy to change attitude and attitude is a big part of civility.

---

[22] "Leadership and Management Training - BusinessBalls.com," Leadership and Management Training - BusinessBalls.com, http://www.businessballs.com/. issues or damages arising from the use of this tool.

[23] "Hardiness Test," Welcome to Queendom! Would you like to learn more about yourself? You've come to the right place!, http://www.queendom.com/tests/access_page/index.htm?idRegTest=700

[24] "Self-Assessment," The American Institute of Stress, June 16, 2020, http://www.stress.org/self-assessment/

[25] "Assessing Your Organization's Learning Culture," Learning to be great, http://www.learningtobegreat.com/assessing-your-organizations-learning-culture

E—evaluated; do we have an evaluation plan in place? How will we know we have met our goals? How will we know which aspects worked and which did not?

R—rewarded; what are the benefits to the employee when he or she exhibits this positive behavior? How can you ensure the benefits will be experienced? What are the benefits to the organization? For example, goes to return on investment.

Assessment Process Phase 3: If conditions were not ideal for any of the four factors, we would conduct further assessment in the identified foundational area. We do this to better understand the factors influencing civility in the organization, and we want to have a clearer view of where we can address any or all of these four conditions. In this way, we lay a foundation for success—and then we can start our civility training in one or more of four civility competency areas—this is our discussion in Chapter 7. However, it must be stated that sometimes, once you address the condition—and/ or restore one or more of the influencing conditions to *ideal* status, you could find that the behaviors or issues you set out to address have been resolved. If the symptoms of incivility have been alleviated, it may be that no civility training is actually required.

To recap:

- A needs assessment is a systematic exploration of the way things are and the way they should be. These *things* are usually associated with organizational and/or individual performance[26].
- The purpose of conducting a needs assessment is to better understand the reason why things are the way they are— rather than the way they should be and how we want them to be. Analyzing the issues and factors that are creating the current situation helps us know what the solution is to get us where we want to be, and where, when, and how we will apply that solution.

---

[26] http://alumnus.caltech.edu/~rouda/T1_HRD.html

- One of the key reasons a needs assessment is completed prior to launching a training plan is to manage resources.
- There are two typical approaches to completing a workplace civility assessment:
  1. Help people identify performance issues and consider what skills gaps are causing the issues as well as how planned training can help to solve them.
  2. Taking a big picture view of the whole organization. Consider current, present, and future activities and goals, and then develop training plans to meet the identified current and anticipated training needs.
- The recommended assessment process is:
  - Phase 1: Complete a general organizational culture assessment.
  - Phase 2: If general organizational culture assessment identifies issues related to incivility, administer assessments to identify which one or more of the four civility culture conditions: readiness, change, alignment, and engagement, is not ideal.
  - Phase 3: When one or more of the four civility culture conditions has been identified as not ideal, conduct further targeted assessments in that specific foundational area.
- One of the ways the compass can save organizations' time and money is because sometimes once the influencing conditions are restored to *ideal*, the incivility symptom is resolved and no training is necessary.

Test Yourself

1. What is not a part of SMARTER goal setting?
   a. Specific
   b. Measurable
   c. *Artistic*
   d. Teachable

2. What is step one of the assessment procedure?
   a. Complete a financial report to see if the company can afford this assessment
   b. *Complete a general organizational culture assessment*
   c. Complete an IQ assessment of all employees
   d. All of the above
3. How do employees express that they are in a high trust workplace?
   a. They feel empowered
   b. They have a shared sense of purpose
   c. They feel empowered to make decisions
   d. *All of the above*

CHAPTER 7

The Civility Competency Matrix

You can't talk yourself out of a problem you've behaved yourself into.
—Stephen R. Covey

As per Covey's words of wisdom, if civility is a problem in your workplace, just talking about it is not likely going to resolve your issues. Discourse certainly has its place, but when habits are ingrained, expectations not clearly defined, and/or when people do not know what they do not know, training is how to solve the problem.

The Civility Culture Compass® outlines four conditions, which when met, increase the likelihood that efforts to build a culture of civility will be successful. The compass also depicts four key skills that collectively

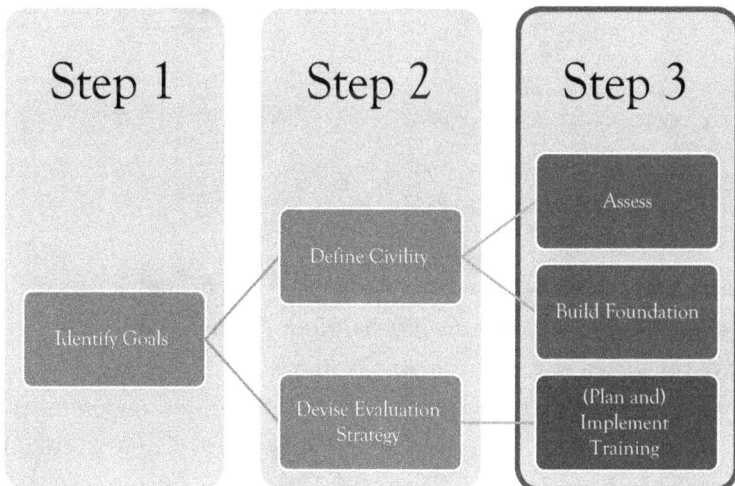

Figure 7.1

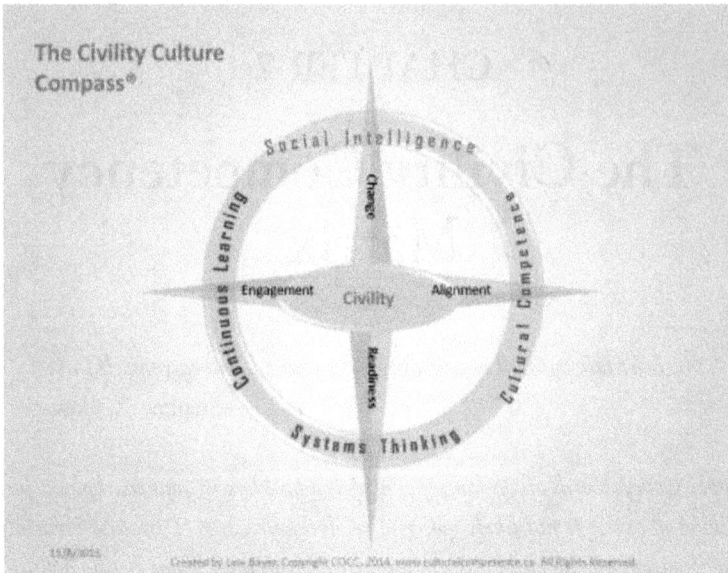

Figure 7.2

make up the overall competency in civility. These are the skill areas in which training is planned and implemented.

Four Key Skills Areas for Competency in Civility

The four key skill areas identified as required for competency in civility are:

- Continuous learning
- Social intelligence (SI)
- Systems thinking
- Cultural competence

The identification of these four skills as key to an individual's ability to exhibit civility at work was based on the review of projects we have completed at Civility Experts Worldwide over the past 17 years. After analyzing outcomes—we use the Kirkpatrick evaluation model (see Chapter 9 for information on this), we started to see patterns emerge. And, we were able to identify clusters of skills that seemed to correlate with exhibition of civility as defined by Civility Experts

Worldwide. We offer more detail on this process in the Civility Competency Matrix® Train the Trainer Program.

- *A **conscious awareness** of the impact of one's thoughts, actions, words, and intentions on others; combined with;*
- *A **continuous acknowledgment** of one's responsibility to ease the experience of others (e.g., through restraint, kindness, non-judgment, respect, and courtesy); and*
- *A **consistent effort** to adopt and exhibit civil behavior as a non-negotiable point of one's character.*

As outlined in Chapter 2, the definition is important, as it describes *exactly* what success will look like. As a result, we are able to identify behavior that results in this success, and we can measure the extent to which the behaviors are exhibited, and how and when, and by whom. And, if we can measure the skill, we can then measure it prior and post training. And, when the learning is transferred to the workplace, we can determine the impact on the workplace.

From the Field: Patterns of Impact—Civility Training at Work

In reviewing projects where we saw a transfer of learning to the workplace after civility training, some of the patterns that emerged were:

Civility Competency Matrix—Overview

The Civility Competency Matrix® is a training tool that details the knowledge, skills, and abilities for each of the four key skill areas that build competency in civility. Training supports and curriculum are customized for organizations. These solutions are based on the matrix and on the organizational assessment outcomes.

The matrix also outlines four competence-based roles—because, as you may recall in Chapter 4, building a culture of civility is best managed as a change initiative. And, a best practice for change initiatives includes assigning a change management team.

Civility-Related Training; Skill Area	Measurable Impact to the Organization
Continuous Learning	- Culture of learning indicators increased e.g., quicker transition to roles, "stickiness" of training, more participation in nonassigned learning - Change readiness indicators increased, e.g., less resistance to change, fewer stress and sick days taken - Employees self-assessed as more resilient, e.g., better able to cope independently - Employees self-assessed as self-identifying skill gaps, e.g., understood value of ongoing learning, actively sought out training - Decreased dependency by employees for organization to manage all learning, e.g., individuals self-directed more often including off-site learning, engaged in mentorship activities - Postevaluation showed reduced overall fear of change, e.g., fewer negative comments, increased trust (verified by survey) and self-increased confidence to overcome barriers,(managers reported less coaching required)
Social Intelligence	- Increased abilities (individually assessed) to interpret verbal, tonal, contextual and nonverbal cues correctly, e.g., ability to predict and/or identify when context created conflict versus individuals choosing it - Employees self-identified social style and were able to adapt same if/as required, e.g., choose to adopt style favored by another - Increased understanding of the written and the unwritten rules of the workplace, e.g., recognize when expectations were not being met based on what was not said or written

Figure 7.3

Civility-Related Training; Skill Area	Measurable Impact to the Organization
Cultural Competence	- Increased understanding of influencing contextual factors, e.g., shift work results in certain workplace culture nuances, male-dominated work group results in certain workplace culture nuances - Decreased fearfulness related to diversity, gender, and generations at work, e.g., self-identifying bias, stereotypes, prejudices that were perceptions versus reality - Increased recognition of shared vision, e.g., that each individual has value
Systems Thinking	- Increased productivity, less wasted resources due to increased alignment, e.g., individuals and teams showed greater accountability to each other and organization; increased recognition of interdependencies

Figure 7.3 (Continued)

Overview
Civility culture compass; competency matrix

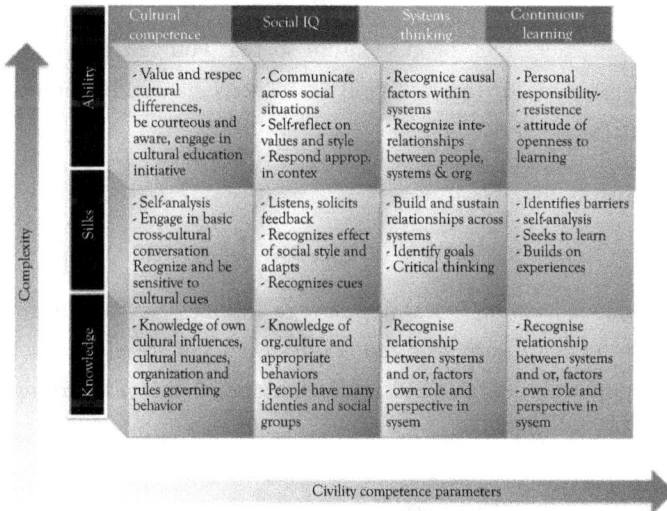

	Cultural competence	Social IQ	Systems thinking	Continuous learning
Ability	- Value and respec cultural differences, be courteous and aware, engage in cultural education initiative	- Communicate across social situations - Self-reflect on values and style - Respond approp. in contex	- Recognice causal factors within systems - Recognize inte-relationships between people, systems & org	- Personal responsibility- - resistence - attitude of openness to learning
Silks	- Self-analysis - Engage in basic cross-cultural conversation Reognize and be sensitive to cultural cues	- Listens, solicits feedback - Recognizes effect of social style and adapts - Recognizes cues	- Build and sustain relationships across systems - Identify goals - Critical thinking	- Identifies barriers - self-analysis - Seeks to learn - Builds on experiences
Knowledge	- Knowledge of own cultural influences, cultural nuances, organization and rules governing behavior	- Knowledge of org.culture and appropriate behaviors - People have many identies and social groups	- Recognise relationship between systems and or, factors - own role and perspective in sysem	- Recognise relationship between systems and or, factors - own role and perspective in sysem

Complexity →

Civility competence parameters →

Figure 7.4

Level 1—Ambassador

Ambassadors are learning; about themselves, their team-mates, about the organization, about civility generally and about the initiative. The goal—engagement, learning, and trust.

Level 2—Coach

Coaches are supporting and guiding the ambassadors. Supports may include providing civility-oriented information, tools, opportunities, and activities to leverage engagement, and so on. Goal—empowerment, skill-building, and change readiness. You have to be an ambassador before you can coach.

Level 3—Change-Maker

Change-makers are directing and managing the initiative/change; only coaches can become change-makers. Goal—strategic plan, standards, and direction toward desired outcome.

Level 4—Exemplar

Exemplars are envisioning and leading. Goal—inspiration, alignment, and collective change.

In this chapter, we are just providing an overview of the four key skills. If you are interested in learning more, or you would like a site license, trainer's kits, or curriculum so that you can deliver training in one or more of the four skill areas, see Chapter 10, Sources and Resources.

About Continuous Learning

Continuous learning is learning how to learn. Every day presents new opportunities to learn from our experiences, but to take advantage of these opportunities, we need to develop our continuous learning skills, including being able to:

- Think in different ways
- Self-reflect
- Inquire and ask questions
- Seek feedback from others

- Draw conclusions
- Gather insights
- Conceptualize the learning process
- Organize our learning
- Participate in training
- Set goals
- Actively engage in gathering knowledge
- Understand our learning style
- Practice applying what we learn
- Adapt and change
- Improve ourselves on an ongoing basis

Blogger Charles Jennings says that "…continuous learning is the only sustainable asset in a world of constant change"[1]. I would agree with this statement. If you are not willing to learn ongoing, you simply will not thrive in the new world of work. Continuous learning benefits individuals by building confidence, increasing competency, improving performance, and enabling future opportunities.

Continuous learning also brings measurable benefits to organizations. For example, in organizations that support a culture of continuous learning, there are often higher levels of engagement, greater accountability, increased cooperation, high productivity, and reduced turnover—this is because in part to increased trust and a mutual understanding by both the employer and the employee that continuous learning increases employability.

There is also a bottom-line benefit of continuous learning, in that organizations with skilled workers have a competitive advantage and usually manage change, as well as the costs often associated with managing change, more effectively than organizations that do not support a culture of continuous learning. One of the key outcomes of continuous learning is that individuals become *knowledge workers*.

---

[1] Jennings, C. 2011. "In a Complex World, Continuous Learning and Simple Truths Prevail." *In a Complex World, Continuous Learning and Simple Truths Prevail,* https://charles-jennings.blogspot.com/2011/10/in-complex-world-continuous-learning.html

Knowledge worker—definition: An individual who *thinks for a living*—that is, he or she values and develops thinking skills and continuous learning habits that enable him or her to be creative, innovative, and forward-thinking. Knowledge workers are effective problem solvers who recognize challenges as opportunities. Knowledge workers analyze the situation at hand and question when appropriate, are constantly learning and growing, and are confident they have, or can, acquire knowledge needed to be successful. Knowledge workers forge ahead in a positive, open-minded, information-seeking and gathering way that enables them to be resilient, adaptive, and ready for change. They embody excellent continuous learning skills, the foundation of a change management mindset[2].

The specific aspects of continuous learning that help an individual exhibit civility are:

- Self-identifying their own learning styles, the learning style of their immediate supervisor and other colleagues.
- Recognizing the components of learning culture that exist in the workplace.
- Considering the nature of change and how change can or will impact their ability to do their job ongoing.
- Becoming aware of the overall organizational adaptive capacity, for example, what does the big picture look like? Is the individual, team, leadership, and so on able and willing to adapt as necessary?

How specifically does continuous learning relate to civility?

In organizations where incivility is assessed as high, we frequently find low adaptive capacity overall. We also see that the organizational culture (for example, hierarchy, policies) may actually inhibit an individual's ability to self-direct, to develop, and/or to learn on the job. Some workplaces actually discourage thinking, and learning is not rewarded. Under these conditions, people tend to develop poor habits, they can become

---

[2] Bayer, H.W. 2011. *Workplace Education Manitoba*. The Change Imperative.

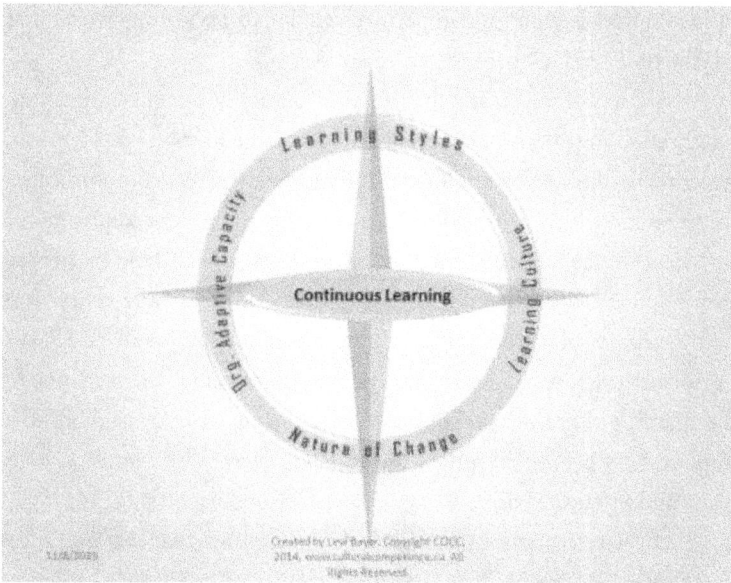

Figure 7.5

complacent, they do not adapt to change well, and this causes resentment, boredom, closed-mindedness, and fearfulness that can manifest as uncivil behavior. If employees are unhappy and disengaged, if they do not feel valued, and there is no incentive to grow, they are frequently not welcoming of new employees or other workplace changes.

About Systems Thinking

Systems thinking is the ability to see the big picture and to distinguish patterns instead of conceptualizing change as isolated events. Systems thinking requires a paradigm shift—from being unconnected to interconnected to the whole, and from blaming our problems on something external to a realization that how we operate, our actions, can create problems[3]. While it might seem obvious to think about the systems, research indicates that we simply are not thinking like we used to. Many experts attribute this decline to an overdependence on technology, others blame

---

[3] Senge, P.M. 1990. *The Fifth Discipline: the Art and Practice of the Learning Organization*. New York, NY: Doubleday.

lifestyle shifts, heightened competitiveness due to a widening world market, the pace of change, or increased stress.

An unprecedented study that followed several thousand undergraduates through four years of college found that large numbers did not learn the critical thinking, complex reasoning, and written communication skills that are widely assumed to be at the core of a college education.

Many of the students graduated without knowing how to sift fact from opinion, make a clear written argument, or objectively review conflicting reports of a situation or event, according to New York University sociologist Richard Arum, lead author of the study. The students, for example, could not determine the cause of an increase in neighborhood crime or how best to respond without being swayed by emotional testimony and political spin.

Arum, whose book *Academically Adrift: Limited Learning on College Campuses* (University of Chicago Press) comes out very soon, followed 2,322 traditional-age students from the fall of 2005 to the spring of 2009 and examined testing data and student surveys at a broad range of 24 U.S. colleges and universities, from the highly selective to the less selective.

In total, 45 percent of the students made no significant improvement in their critical thinking, reasoning, or writing skills during the first two years of college, according to the study. After four years, 36 percent showed no significant gains in these so-called *higher-order* thinking skills.

Systems thinking requires:

- A clear understanding of the organizational goals
- An understanding of the internal and external systems that are impacting the organization (at a macro level, the systems impacting the community, and the sector, and the world economy, and so on; and at a micro level, the systems impacting the department, the team, and the individual)
- An understanding of the networks—the connections, interrelationships, and interdependencies influencing the systems
- Ongoing understanding of the specific workplace environment and related conditions

How specifically does systems thinking relate to civility?

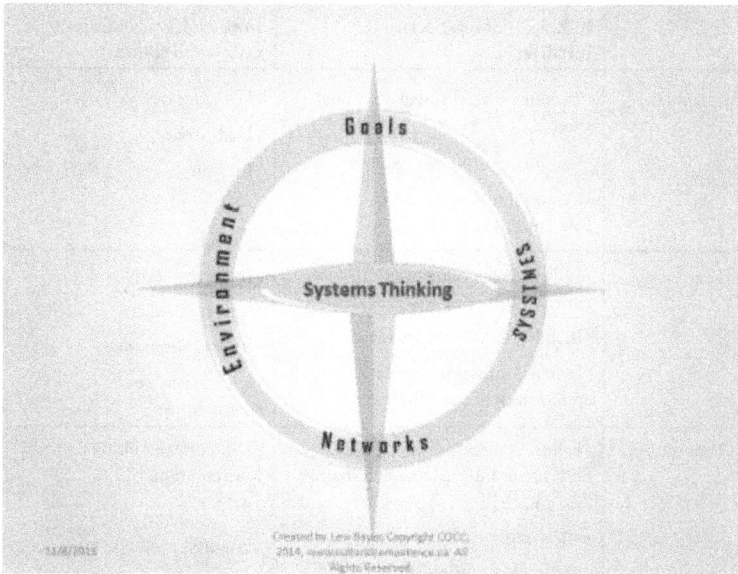

Figure 7.6

When people are not able to see how they fit into the big picture, they tend to become confused, disillusioned, and disengaged. When they do not see interconnectedness, they feel separate and tend to blame and make assumptions about how and why things are happening. This can result in learned helplessness, victim syndromes, passive (and overt) aggression, and, most damaging of all, mistrust. When trust goes, respect follows close behind, and all sorts of incivility happens.

About Social Intelligence

According to Karl Albrecht, researcher and author of *Social Intelligence - The New Science of Success*, SI is in the simplest terms, "The ability to get along with people." It is assumed that people acquire this skill experientially as they grow up, mature, and gain experience in dealing with others. Unfortunately, many people do not continue to learn and grow as they age, and many never acquire the awareness and skills they need to succeed in social, business, or professional situations. SI underpins our ability to have good judgment in interpersonal interactions and across a range of social settings. As such *common sense* and *having a sense of people* are what happens when you actually use your SI.

	Indicators of low Social Intelligence	Impact (degree of impact varies with context)
Individual	- Inability to read verbal and tonal cues - Inability to exercise restraint - Communication faux pa. e.g., Interrupting, ignoring	- Low confidence - High stress - Incivility
Team	- Failure to see value in contribution of others - Inability to adapt to change - Increased miscommunication and/or lack of communication	- Ineffective teamwork - Low resilience - Poor performance - Lack of service orientation
Organization	- Failure to identify demographic Shifts both internal and external - Inability to create an empowering environment - Difficulty fostering "fit"	- Difficulty recruiting and/or low retention - Poor engagement - Lowered productivity

Figure 7.7

Current research shows that SI has declined significantly over the last decade. The reasons for this include, among other things: parenting style shifts, generational and cultural issues, trends, and reliance on technology. At present, how we have become so socially incompetent is not as important as what we are going to do about it. This, because our inability to interact successfully, can have devastating consequences. A few examples outlined in the following show how low SI can impact us at work.

The good news is that psychologists have identified that SI can be improved; we can actually teach it. And, our ability to teach it effectively enables us to meet the demands of increasingly diverse, ever-changing workplaces. In the new world of work—where collaboration may well be considered currency—SI, is absolutely essential to success.

In terms of ability to exhibit civility, there are four elements of SI that are important:

- Social radar; ability to correctly interpret nonverbal and contextual cues
- Social style, and specifically the ability to adapt one's style
- Social knowledge, of the written and the unwritten rules

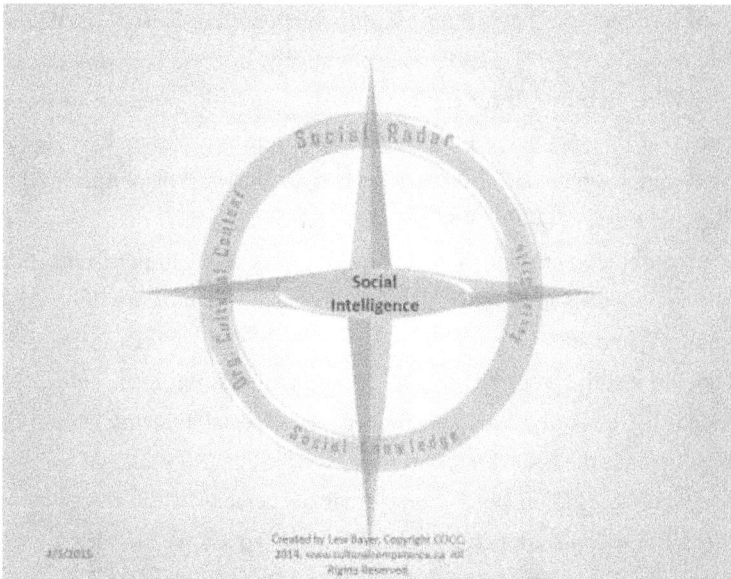

Figure 7.8

- Understanding of the social expectations specific to the workplace; the nuances of the organizational cultural context

How specifically does SI relate to civility?
There is a cluster of behaviors that collectively make up SI; they are:

- Paying attention
- Focusing on someone or something other than oneself
- Connecting with others in a meaningful way
- Being aware of our surroundings
- Thinking about what might be appropriate in a certain context
- Consciously adapting behavior to show consideration and respect for others
- Considering the impact of our words and actions
- Seeking to understand expectations for social behavior in different contexts
- Exhibiting common courtesies; meeting general social expectations

This cluster of behaviors represents habits that socially successful people engage in. When a person does not engage in these behaviors, he or she may be perceived as rude. Frequently, people with low SI are not even aware that they are being perceived as rude, and often, they have developed inappropriate social habits. Related to the workplace specifically, Albrecht, (*Social IQ-The New Science of Success*) suggests that low social radar combined with poor social knowledge can result in persistent rude behaviors he calls *toxic*. Toxic and disrespectful behaviors are often contagious. When allowed to do so, rudeness spreads like a virus and wreaks havoc on health, productivity, self-esteem, and relationships. Left unattended, the incivility virus quickly becomes a social epidemic, at which point treating the behavioral symptoms is barely manageable. Given that recent public opinion polls showed that 69 percent of the respondents agreed that people are getting ruder, it is safe to say we are facing incivility in epidemic proportions. (See Chapter 9, Tools You Can Use, for a toxicity survey.)

About Cultural Competence

A geographically dispersed, culturally diverse workforce and marketplace is the new reality. Global businesses and organizations need people who can work effectively in cultural diversity and to create an environment that promotes mutual respect and creative collaboration.

Exposure to new cultures and to multicultural social networks and teams in a workplace is more likely to have positive consequences if those involved have been properly trained to understand and appreciate fundamental cultural differences and values that impact workplace relationships. Factors such as communication style, management style, and approaches to diversity and inclusion are as varied as cultures.

The way forward is cultural competence; this includes:

- Learning about our own culture, our own biases, and attitudes
- Recognizing and understanding differences (real and perceived) in behaviors, beliefs, styles of work, and styles of communicating
- Being sensitive to identified differences

- Communicating effectively and working together with people who are different than we are

Cultural competence is not easy to achieve. By way of a cultural continuum[4], Arredondo suggests there are six stages. The first of these is *cultural destructiveness* (see Chapter 9). And, this is the level where we see heightened incivility in workplaces.

Steven Covey states, "Strength lies in differences, not similarities." And, we find this to be true in organizations. When we can capitalize on what makes us different—we each bring our own unique strengths and perspectives to the table at work—and with enough skills and knowledge, we can harness these differences to create something even better. A better team, a better product, a better company, a better world. The goal of cultural competence in the workplace is to create a sense of community such that we can build *citizenship*. In his book *Community*, Peter Block describes citizenship as follows:

Citizenship is a state of being. It is a choice for activism and care. A citizen is one who is willing to do the following:

- Hold oneself accountable for the well-being of the larger collective of which we are a part.
- Choose to own and exercise power rather than to defer or delegate it to others.
- Enter into a collective possibility that gives a workplace community its own sense of being.
- Acknowledge that the community grows out of the possibility of citizens. Community is built not by specialized expertise, or great leadership, or improved services; it is built by great citizens.
- Attend to the gifts and capacities of all others, and act to bring the gifts of those on the margin into the center[5].

---

[4] Arredondo, E. 1970. "Cultural Competence." *SpringerLink*. Springer, New York, NY. https://link.springer.com/referenceworkentry/10.1007/978-1-4419-1005-9_172

[5] Peter, B. 2008. *Community the Structure of Belonging*. San Francisco, CA: Berrett-Koehler Publishers Inc. a BK Business book.

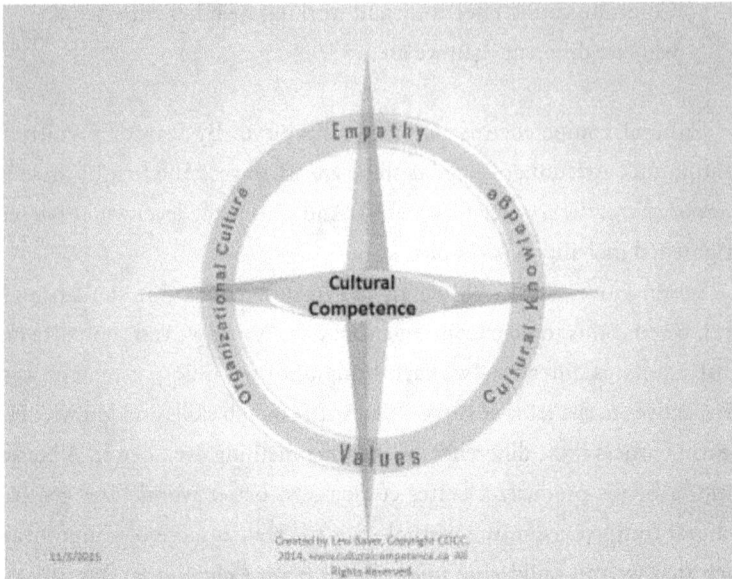

Figure 7.9

Developing skills in cultural competence requires:

- Empathy—Knowing what it is and how to recognize and exhibit it.
- Cultural knowledge, for example, about the diverse groups that may be represented in your organization.
- Values—Specifically that you understand your own values, the organizational values, and the values of others. This because for most people, our values underpin our motivations and drive our decision making.
- Organizational culture—Every organization has a culture of its own, and you really have to experience it to understand it. Also, culture changes as the people in the culture change, and so, these elements of cultural competence are very difficult to achieve.

How specifically does SI relate to civility?

When civility assessments show low tolerance for diversity, high mistrust, conflict, poor team orientation and high turnover, we often find that the causal factors relate to low cultural competence. There has been a lot of change in workplaces in terms of demographics; more people of culture, more women in leadership positions, up to four generations working together, and so on, and when people are stressed or fearful due to change, they tend to default to their weaker selves. Biases, stereotypes, and prejudices tend to come forward. People make assumptions and presume the worst of each other. Because we focus on differences, mistrust and self-preservation take over, and we behave badly. Because communication is sometimes hindered, individuals do not have the opportunity to discover that we are more alike than we are different. Often, we have the same values but different habits or traditions, and so, outward behaviors are not reflective of the inner workings and motivations. If we can find a way to engage in a discussion about values, and if we can teach people to focus on the sameness, we remove the mistrust and fearfulness, and most people will extend kindness and respect.

Recommended Homework

- If civility is a problem in your workplace, talking about it is not likely going to resolve your issues. Discourse certainly has its place, but when habits are ingrained, expectations not clearly defined, and/or when people do not know what they do not know, training is how to solve the problem. Create an assessment plan to identify civility issues in your workplace (or a workplace you choose).
- The Civility Culture Compass® outlines four conditions, which when met, increase the likelihood that efforts to build a culture of civility will be successful. The compass also depicts four key skills that collectively make up overall competency in civility. These are the skill areas in which training is planned and implemented. Which skills can you identify as a need for training based on your assessment?
- The Civility Competency Matrix® is a training tool that details the knowledge, skills, and abilities for each of the four key skill areas that build competency in civility. These skill areas are:
  - Continuous learning—Learning strategies for learning ongoing

- SI—Ability to effectively identify and interpret nonverbal, verbal, and contextual cues, to adapt social style, and to apply written and unwritten social rules—this enables you to get along with others
- Systems thinking—The ability to see the big picture, to distinguish patterns, to recognize interconnectedness of the systems, and to see your role within the systems
- Cultural competence—Being able to appreciate fundamental cultural differences and values that impact workplace relationships, and doing so in a way that benefits the parties involved and leverages differences—real or imagined
- Training in one or more of these four key skills areas under *ideal* conditions can result in measurable impact to the bottom line. Devise learning objectives and a training plan to address the civility skill gaps you identifed for your organization.

Test Yourself

1. Continuous learning involves the ability to....
   a. Set goals
   b. Self-reflect
   c. Gather insights
   d. All of the above and more
2. Systems thinking is...
   a. Computer operating systems that allow a business to function
   b. The ability to see the bigger picture and view connections and patterns
   c. Encouraging others
   d. Creating elaborate plans and proposals
3. In simplest terms, SI is...
   a. Knowing how to manipulate people
   b. Having a large social network
   c. Being outgoing and personable
   d. The ability to get along with other people

CHAPTER 8

Putting It All Together

How to Build a Culture of Civility in Your Organization

1. Identify problems and issues in your workplace.
   Recommend: Use the Symptoms of Incivility Survey; identify any of the symptoms you are experiencing in your workplace.
2. Choose your *hedgehog concept*, for example, choose civility.
3. Determine the *end in mind*. Set a goal related to the specific change you want to see. Expand the goal using SMARTER formula. For example, goal: assess and address competency gaps in continuous learning skills of all employees (200) in XYZ division by December 31, 20XX. Transfer of learning will be measured by comparing pre- and post-training trust levels. If successful, we will see at least a 10 percent increase in employee retention in our XYZ division.
   S (specific)
   M (measured)
   A (attainable or attained by)
   R (realistic)
   T (timed or timing)
   E (evaluated)
   R (return on investment or reward)
4. Identify indicators of success and determine how you will measure these indicators.
5. Use the Civility Culture Compass to identify the extent to which each of four conditions that support a successful civility change initiative are *ideal*. These conditions are:
   a. Change
   b. Alignment
   c. Engagement
   d. Readiness

6. Once you have ensured the conditions are right, begin to assess competency in the four key areas that support a culture of civility; these are:
   a. Social intelligence
   b. Continuous learning
   c. Systems thinking
   d. Cultural competence
7. Devise a training plan based on the outcomes of your assessment. The plan will include:
   a. Learning objectives
   b. Evaluation strategy
8. Assign a change initiative team to manage the change. There are four main roles on the team:
   a. Exemplar
   b. Change-maker
   c. Coach
   d. Ambassador
9. Roll out the change or learning plan.
10. Evaluate outcomes.
11. Revisit the four conditions on the Civility Culture Compass ongoing and adjust as necessary.
12. Adjust roles and goals ongoing.
13. Track successes and setbacks.
14. Reward civility—celebrate organizational culture change.

Eating an Elephant

At a glance, it can seem that building a culture of civility is a tremendous undertaking. However, it is well worth the effort to engage in this important endeavor. (In Chapter 1, we talked about all the possible positive outcomes of civility training.) Once you have identified that there is a problem (in Chapter 6, we talked about how to assess general civility in your workplace), you just need to commit to start. And, if you cannot take on a comprehensive civility initiative, why not start with one bite?

I can tell you from 18 years of experience in the field that civility training results in, or is at least, a contributing factor in achieving each and every one of the following outcomes. So, if you have limited time or resources, and/or if you cannot do a comprehensive assessment, it is recommended that you choose just one positive outcome from the following list. Choose something that is important in your specific workplace. Check the condition indicated in italic. (These are the conditions that our research and experience show to be most likely to impact the outcome indicated. And then, once you have addressed that condition, *if* the problem has not resolved itself, then you would build competency in the skill area(s) recommended (indicated by an arrow) for that outcome.) (While all four skills overlap, we have found some outcomes readily and consistently tied to one or two of the skills.) In this way, you can take a shortcut and go directly to training in a key area and still experience the benefits of civility in your workplace.

- Increased retention *Engagement*
  - Continuous learning, systems thinking
- Greater individual and organizational adaptive capacity *Readiness or change*
  - Continuous learning, cultural competence
- Employee autonomy *Engagement*
  - Continuous learning, systems thinking
- Individual skills mastery and increased confidence *Readiness or change*
  - Cultural competence, social intelligence
- More effective goal-setting *Alignment*
  - Systems thinking, continuous learning
- Better alignment of daily activity with organizational goals *Alignment*
  - Cultural competence, systems thinking
- More accountability *Alignment*
  - Social intelligence, cultural competence
- Increased safety *Engagement*
  - Social intelligence, systems thinking
- Greater consistency in service delivery *Change*
  - Social intelligence, cultural competence, systems thinking

- Increased respect in the workplace *Engagement*
  - All skills contribute
- More frequent exhibition of common courtesies *Engagement*
  - Social intelligence
- Generalized reciprocity *Alignment*
  - Cultural competence
- More civil discourse *Readiness*
  - Cultural competence, systems thinking
- More efficient communication *Engagement or **a**lignment*
  - Social intelligence, cultural competence
- Increased acceptance of diversity *Readiness or change*
  - Cultural competence, social intelligence, continuous learning
- Greater team-orientation *Engagement*
  - Systems thinking, cultural competence
- More collaboration *Engagement or alignment*
  - Social intelligence, cultural competence, systems thinking

Highlights From the Chapters

- Civility in the workplace is an issue all around the world.
- There is an increasing body of research suggesting that incivility in the workplace is systemic and epidemic, and it is time for a change.
- To successfully imbed civility into your workplace culture, it is necessary to approach civility in the workplace as a change initiative.
- While a respectful workplace policy may be required, and can be useful, the policy in and of itself does not guarantee a respectful workplace.
- 70 percent of change initiatives fail.
- Engagement is essential to facilitating lasting, meaningful culture change, and in order for a civility initiative to be successful, organizations must be *change-ready* skills-wise. This means employees must be competent in four skill areas that underpin the ability to exhibit civility at work.

- The first step in the three-step civility plan is to have an end in mind. Goal-setting is based on this desired outcome, and your SMARTER goal will drive the civility initiative process.
- Civility Experts Worldwide defines civility as:
  - A *conscious awareness* of the impact of one's thoughts, actions, words, and intentions on others; combined with,
  - A *continuous acknowledgment* of one's responsibility to ease the experience of others (for example, through restraint, kindness, nonjudgment, respect, and courtesy); and,
  - A *consistent effort* to adopt and exhibit civil behavior as a non-negotiable point of one's character.
- There is growing evidence that civility can have tremendous positive and measurable impacts on organizations, including:
  - Engagement, morale, and retention
  - Confidence, continuous learning, and competency
  - Respect, restraint, and responsibility
  - Psychological safety, stress management, and resilience
  - Change readiness, adaptive capacity, and profitability
- Step 2 in the process for creating a workplace civility initiative has two substeps: Substep 1 is to define civility. Your definition should support your *hedgehog concept*, which is to choose civility, so that it will likely be an expanded SMARTER version of a basic goal to *build a better workplace*. The definition must be specific to your workplace context, and you must include behavioral indicators; these are descriptions of what exactly civility looks like on the job.
- Substep 2 is to devise an evaluation strategy. You have to define civility—so you know exactly what behaviors you are looking for, before you can outline a strategy for evaluating whether or not, and how, those behaviors are being exhibited, and whether or not, and how, this is benefiting the organization.
- Civility is not the same as courtesy, or the same as manners, or etiquette; these are all related but different.
- A civility initiative is a change imperative for companies that want to thrive in the new world of work.

- Companies that openly promote civil communication among employees earn 30 percent more revenue than competitors, are four times more likely to have highly engaged employees, and are 20 percent more likely to report reduced turnover[1].
- If an increase in revenue is not incentive enough, there are two other issues to consider when you need to persuade your leadership or team to support your civility initiative; they are:
  i. How to get over the *civility = manners = soft skills, and soft skills are nice to have but not necessary skills* hurdle
  ii. What will convince your team that civility training is worthwhile—will it be the costs, benefits, or consequences of civility or incivility in the workplace?
- Your ability to explain what civility is relative to skills and competencies at work, combined with your ability to identify which proven outcomes of civility will be most meaningful to your stakeholders, will impact the likelihood that your organization will choose civility. Some helpful information in this regard is as follows:
  o There is increasing evidence that skills once presumed to be *soft* or nice to have are, in fact, critical to long-term success.
  o Soft skills can be described as a cluster of personal qualities related to willingness, attitude, personality, and social intelligence.
  o Soft skills incorporate *essential skills*—these are the skills and abilities needed for work, learning, and life. Essential skills provide the foundation for learning all other skills and enable people to evolve with their jobs and adapt to workplace change.
  o Exhibiting civility requires incorporating a range of soft and essential skills in different combinations.
  o Research shows that the majority of one's financial success is because of skills in *human engineering*. Human engineering includes elements of your personality and your ability

---

[1] "Civility in America 2011." *Weber Shandwick*, https://webershandwick.com/news/civility-in-america-2011/

to communicate, negotiate, and lead. Human engineering is less reliant on technical knowledge, as previously understood, and more reliant on soft skills.

- There is evidence that civility in the workplace results in:
  - Increased revenue and engagement
  - Increased morale, physical and mental health, and happiness at work
  - Increased team orientation and ability to work well with others
  - Increased performance and productivity
- To survive and to thrive in the new world, and the new world of work, we need to learn continuously, and we need to learn at the pace of change.
- To be competent in the four skills (social intelligence, continuous learning, cultural competence, and systems thinking) that build a culture of civility and/or enable an individual to exercise civility ongoing, you need to be able to adapt to change.
- When managed properly, the stress of change can be positive, for example, cause the human brain to use more of its capabilities, improve memory, and intelligence, and even increase productivity.
- Change can be frightening, but it is not so scary if you change your perspective and see it as an opportunity to learn.
- You do not need a grand launch or a catchy tagline for your civility initiative.
- The crisis has already happened, incivility is likely already impacting your bottom line.
- Fear is not a good motivator—for a lot of things, but especially not when it comes to fostering civility.
- Building a culture of civility does not have to be an abrupt, painful process. When done properly, making the change from uncivil to civil is a continuous process where small, subtle, painless processes enable people to think and act differently.
- Take a page from Jim Collins book *Good to Great*—literally. Be a hedgehog not a fox. If your goal is to build a better workplace, choose civility—that is your hedgehog concept.

- Learning to be civil is at first an experiential exercise, that is, our attitudes about kindness, and respect, and compassion, and graciousness, and generosity, and so on, develop as a result of our childhood experiences and upbringing.
- In many workplaces, the pull toward incivility gets stronger because:
  - Choosing incivility is easier than choosing civility.
  - There are more rewards than consequences for being uncivil.
  - We are not learning to be civil through our experiences and interactions at work, and without experiencing civility, it is difficult to understand the benefits of it.
  - The written and unwritten rules have changed so much, and are changing constantly, and so many of us just are not sure of the current expectations, so we mirror the behavior of whomever seems to be leading at a specific time, in a specific context.
  - Civility in the workplace has been dismissed for a very long time as something *nice to have*, and so, civility is rarely strategically or formally taught.
  - Even when they know what civility is, many people simply do not have the skills they need to exhibit civility in an ever-changing workplace.
- In a workplace context, where incivility can be attributed to a lack of experiential education, the plan for fostering a culture civility in the workplace is to change their experience. We do this by:
  - Creating an environment where positive change (learning) is required and supported—this is to replace an environment where bad habits and negativity have been endorsed over positive change or learning
  - Encouraging (and in fact requiring by way of policy and procedure) this positive change in the form of behavior in four key skill areas that underpin an ability to be civil
- The Civility Culture Compass® offers a model for a creating a culture of civility in your workplace. The compass outlines a proactive, competency-based approach to shifting

organizational culture from toxic and negative to respectful and positive. The Civility Culture Compass® is used to assess four organizational conditions, which when *ideal* as described next, increase the success of civility initiatives. These conditions are:

○ Change

○ Alignment

○ Engagement

○ Readiness

- Civility as a core competency requires that an individual can exhibit certain measurable, and related knowledge, skills, abilities, and commitments, and to do so consistently, in a way, and at a standard prescribed for application in a specific context, for example, a workplace, in a way that is deemed effective for that context.

- A needs assessment is a systematic exploration of the way things are and the way they should be. These *things* are usually associated with organizational and/or individual performance[2].

- The purpose of conducting a needs assessment is to better understand the reason why things are the way they are, rather than the way they should be and how we want them to be. Analyzing the issues and factors that are creating the current situation helps us know what the solution is to get us where we want to be, and where, when, and how we will apply that solution.

- One of the key reasons a needs assessment is completed prior to launching a training plan is to manage resources.

- There are two typical approaches to completing a workplace civility assessment:

  ○ Help people identify performance issues and consider what skills gaps are causing the issues as well as how planned training can help to solve them.

---

[2] Robery H. Rouda and Mitchell E. Kusy. "Needs Assessment: The First Step." NEEDS ASSESSMENT the first step, 1995, http://flash.lakeheadu.ca/~mstones/needs_assessment.html

- ○ Taking a big picture view of the whole organization.
  Consider current, present, and future activities and goals,
  and then develop training plans to meet the
  identified current and anticipated training needs.
- The recommended assessment process is:
  - ○ Phase 1: Complete a general organizational culture assessment.
  - ○ Phase 2: If general organizational culture assessment identifies
    issues related to incivility, administer assessments to identify
    which one or more of the four civility culture conditions:
    readiness, change, alignment, and engagement, is not ideal.
  - ○ Phase 3: When one or more of the four civility culture conditions have been identified as not ideal, conduct further
    targeted assessments in that specific foundational area.
- One of the ways the compass can save organizations' time and
  money is because sometimes once the influencing conditions
  are restored to *ideal*, the incivility symptom is resolved, and
  no training is necessary.
- If civility is a problem in your workplace, talking about it is
  not likely going to resolve your issues. Discourse certainly
  has its place, but when habits are ingrained, expectations not
  clearly defined, and/or people do not know what they do not
  know, training is how to solve the problem.
- The Civility Culture Compass® outlines four conditions,
  which when met, increase the likelihood that efforts to build a
  culture of civility will be successful. The compass also depicts
  four key skills that collectively make up overall competency in
  civility. These are the skill areas in which training is planned
  and implemented.
- The Civility Competency Matrix® is a training tool that details
  the knowledge, skills, and abilities for each of the four key skill
  areas that build competency in civility. These skill areas are:
  - ○ Continuous learning—Learning strategies for learning
    ongoing
  - ○ Social intelligence—The ability to effectively identify and
    interpret nonverbal, verbal, and contextual cues, to adapt

social style, and to apply written and unwritten social rules; this enables you to get along with others

- ○ Systems thinking—The ability to see the big picture, to distinguish patterns, to recognize interconnectedness of the systems, and to see your role within the systems
- ○ Cultural competence—Being able to appreciate fundamental cultural differences and values that impact workplace relationships, and doing so in a way that benefits the parties involved and leverages differences—real or imagined
- Training in one or more of these four key skills areas under *ideal* conditions can result in measurable impact to the bottom line.

Sample Workplace Application of the Four Skills

As a way of showing how the civility competencies overlap and tie into an individual's ability to be civil, provided next is an excerpt from Ms. Olen Juarez-Lim, Civility Experts Philippines, AICI FLC on professional presence.

According to Ms. Juarez-Lim, for most business professionals, *presence* relates to an ability to present oneself in a way that conveys credibility and to influence others through your leadership and communication skills. When people are perceived not to have *presence*, it is frequently because they do not show high social intelligence, they do not follow expected social rules, they do not communicate respect, and they seem *me-focused* versus *other-focused*.

Olen (Juarez-Lim recounts an experience.)

I was at a driveway in a client's office building waiting for my car and I noticed a tall, gray-haired man stepping down from his SUV. He was scanning the area with his smile and all of a sudden, people were drawn to him like a rock star. I too was caught in the rapture and all of a sudden I recognized the man as the CEO of the company! I said to myself, "Wow." In less than 15 seconds this man has drawn everyone to his presence.

In gatherings, meetings, and events or just simply out on the street, there is always this one individual people will notice. He or she has a commanding entrance, and an attractiveness that is not overpowering.

He or she engages with a smile and eye contact. When they speak, people listen. They have quiet confidence that suggests when they lead, people follow. They may stop traffic as they cross the street (extreme). There is an allure that is effortlessly echoed like metal being captivated in by a magnet. That is personal presence.

When people are asked to define personal presence, they may refer to it as "I'll know it when I see it," as un-definable, they will call it the X factor. According to *Merriam-Webster dictionary, presence is the fact or condition of being present; the part of space within one's immediate vicinity the bearing, carriage, or air of a person, especially: stately or distinguished bearing or a noteworthy quality of poise and effectiveness (the actor's commanding presence). It is, therefore, attributed to appearance, behavior (appropriate for a context as its mostly positive behaviors we focus on), communication (timely, effective, and thoughtful), and authenticity of a person.

Personal presence is difficult to define, but is easily detected. (We use our social radar to detect it by way of social cues, tone of voice, nonverbal communication, and so on.) It comes in instantaneously, and the effect is powerful. There is something special about people with presence. The way they connect with their eyes as if you are the only person in the room. They speak with much enthusiasm yet not filling the air with noise. They look polished, with poise and confidence, but never arrogance. They have great personality and charm, but never an exaggerated sense of self-importance. They act with a purpose and have grace under pressure. They are trusted and respected and have a natural, unforced quality. They are at ease and inspire the same genuine confidence to influence others positively. This is largely because of social intelligence.

Genuine and authentic, yes this is difficult to fake. Personal presence is the belief we have in ourselves that everything is aligned with—from our nonverbal signals to the energy we put forth, it has to be closely synched that our credibility is built solid. The impact of personal presence helps us achieve our goals and ambitions.

First Impressions

Recently, I purchased a vehicle and went to several car dealerships around my city. Obviously, if I am purchasing something as expensive as a car, I needed to get my money's worth, and I was a hawk when it came to first impressions from the salesperson and the car.

As I entered Car Dealer A, the sales people did not seem to be energetic or enthusiastic about someone buying from them. But, because I was interested in this particular brand, I pursued and ask questions until I finally was assisted to check out the car I want. The sales person was a fairly decent looking young man, had cold hands, and was not too quick in replying to my questions.

Car Dealer B, I was welcomed upon entering, the young lady with quite short skirt and high-pitched voice was enthusiastic to make her sale, always referring to the money value and every car I liked was not on stock.

Car Dealer C was a stretch for me. I was met by a young lady in uniform. She spoke very well and was knowledgeable for the most part, but she did not strike me as particularly special in any way. But, there was no question with the car; it was a dream for me.

Car Dealers A and B failed my first impression test. The first impression one makes has something to do with how you made a person feel at the onset of the first chance meeting.

If there is anything I have learned in life, making a successful impression can come down to a blink of an eye after meeting someone. People will make assumptions based on their perception and will always believe that no matter how much you present them with facts, sadly, they will always refer to the first impression they have of you. We are wired to make quick assumptions about people, and more often, we relate to others similar to us. The conclusions drawn from the observations are surprisingly accurate and lasting.

Malcolm Gladwell in his book *Blink*, describes the type of unconscious thinking called rapid cognition as something that moves quicker and acts mysteriously, gauging what is important from that quick encounter. It is referred to as thin slicing: "Thin-slicing harnesses this powerful adaptive unconsciousness, allowing us to make smart decisions based on minimal information and minimal deliberation*" (Paul Marsden, *Blink Summary: The Power of Thinking Without Thinking*).

This thin-slicing is influenced by our values and our cultural competence. Depending on our experiences, we make judgments and assumptions as well as smart decisions, and it is our continuous learning that enables us to adjust our perceptions and hone our adaptive consciousness.

Thin-slicing is not an exotic gift. It is a central part of what it means to be human. We thin-slice whenever we meet a new person or have to make sense of something quickly or encounter a novel situation. We thin-slice because we have to, and we come to rely on that ability because there are lots of situations where careful attention to the details of a very thin slice, even for no more than a second or two, can tell us an awful lot

—Malcolm Gladwell, Blink.

Therefore, paying attention to the details of how we project ourselves that constitute our first impression is vital. And, it is all about details, details, details. It is the details that separate luxury from inferior, excellence from mediocrity.

What value can we derive from this, knowing that snap judgments are made about us? First is awareness; it allows us to use this information to our advantage, letting us prepare for these interactions. When going for a job interview, it prepares you to project the image you want the employers to see and land that job. Second, it allows us to prepare and practice. Excellence does not happen overnight. It takes practice to connect and use valuable details such as nonverbal communication that ultimately creates big impressions.

How a person presents himself or herself at work (for example, consider the three different car dealers) incorporates all four core skills related to civility:

Social IQ:

- Knowing what is appropriate clothing?
- Being aware of how people respond to one's presence, for example, are they bowled over? Interested? Approaching?
- Knowing what the expectations are for greeting and approaching people
- Knowing when and how to adjust personal style to accommodate needs of others
- Having ability to put focus on others' needs and wants versus one's own

- Being appropriate, for example, watching for cues that a listener may not want to talk about money, or apologizing when it is clear that a customer is distressed about the car he or she wants being out of stock

Cultural competence:

- Recognizing that *appropriate* approach, clothes, tone of voice, and so on vary depending on age, gender, ethnicity, and other aspects
- Choosing not to judge others unfairly based on their outward appearance or behavior
- Awareness of personal biases and perceptions
- Having the ability to assess when a difference makes a difference and then adjusting your behavior accordingly
- Recognizing that individuals, teams, families, communities, cities, countries, and certainly organizations are each cultures within a culture
- Understanding

Continuous learning:

- Being able to learn from mistakes
- Building on existing skills
- Ability to ask questions, for example, when in uncomfortable settings
- Ability to recognize that change requires adjustments

Systems thinking:

- Recognizing that we are all interconnected, for example, someone knows someone who knows someone, so be careful what you say and do
- Understanding that every action on our part is going to impact someone or some system in some way

- Recognizing that we contribute to the current system, and that in our contribution, we are impacting other systems

Best practices from the field, recommended by Olen Juarez-Lim, Master Certified Civility Trainer, Civility Experts Affiliate and Reseller for Philippines; ways to convey civility through your personal image:

Watch Your Attitude

Attitude is everything and self-perception determines direction, that is according to Nick Vujicic, author and inspirational speaker, born with no arms and no legs. His story simply puts things in perspective, the message of faith and hope, displays how our attitude can ultimately lead us to failure or success.

What we declare is what we attract. Our attitude is everything about how we see life, deal with it, and manage it. We cannot control what life brings—the hurdles, trials—but we can control our own attitude towards it. A positive attitude, optimism, and enthusiasm work like a magnet for success and change. One of the earlier books of inspiration I read was Dr. Cherie Carter Scott's book, *If Life is a Game, These are the Rules*, and Rule number 4 always resonates with me: "Lessons are repeated until they are learned"; it clearly defines that each hurdle may be treated as opportunities to learn from. Once we get what the present situation is teaching us, we evolve and change and consciously make decisions not to repeat them.

This process is important for personal success, in that knowing that we are not perfect and have room for improvement, we can make conscious decisions to take care of our brand to get ahead in life. Lessons present us with teachers who will teach us the valuable lesson until we get it right. We may dodge the issue facing us, but rest assured, it will always come back until we face it and learn from it. By shifting your perspective to what value the situation presents, it alters your view of approaching things. It equips you to evaluate things differently, makes you look into the positive sides of things and, ultimately, you grow wiser.

Mirjam Stoffels, founder of sevent2success, said "Positive thinking changes the brain. Positive thinking really does change your brain. In a real physical way. The science is called neuroplasticity. Scientists are proving the brain is endlessly adaptable and dynamic. It means that our thoughts can change the structure and function of our brains. Repetitive positive thought and positive activity can rewire your brain and strengthen brain areas that stimulate positive feelings. The brain can form new neural pathways—if we do the work. Just like exercise, the work requires repetition and activity to reinforce new learning." Therefore, you can tell success by the way you think it. If you tell your mind to feel confident, your body moves confidently.

Be a Person of Character and Authenticity

Personal presence is work from the inside out. No matter how well dressed we are, maneuver the table with precision, or speak well, people can tell if we are sincere or not. Everyone nowadays is sophisticated enough to tell the difference from a sincere smile to a nervous one. Having strong personal values and beliefs that are non-negotiable in developing character and authenticity. It is ingrained from your core and, ultimately, is the barometer from which people gauge your worth. When you know who you are and what you stand for, people believe in you. It acts as a foundation to guide you in making decisions that are true to your beliefs. You act, work, speak your worth. Clients, office mates, employers would always remember how you made them feel.

Hone Your Conversational Skills

The way you communicate, tone of voice, and the energy you put into communicating speaks about your charisma. Speak with certainty and conviction so that it gives you confidence to sell almost anything. Manage your body language, facial expression, and tone of voice, as these contribute greatly to the message being conveyed.

Dress Appropriately

The visual impact we make speaks volumes and comprises about 55 percent of the way we are perceived. Clothes do make an impact—from the fit, to the style, color choice, to the appropriateness of occasion, and how we pay attention to details—it all matters! Our clothes communicate a message, and to get ahead in business, we project that image of trust and confidence. It helps form a mental picture of our first impression, which we know by now, is lasting. Part of the overall visual grade is grooming. Be neat and clean, and be impeccable. From the details of unwanted hair in the nose, or upper lip, to your scent or smell, and the minding the personal details is just pure common sense. Knowing the impact that we create when we meet people, we need to make a conscious effort in taking care of our brand. The way we will be perceived is entirely up to us. The way we are accorded respect is entirely up to us. It may take effort, but I guarantee the rewards are great.

Test Yourself

1. If you are unable to do every element on the checklist to building civility in your workplace, you should:
    a. Avoid trying anything if you cannot do everything
    b. Find the one element that will have the largest impact and start with that
    c. Figure out what will be the cheapest aspect to bring into your workplace and start there
    d. None of the above

2. True or false, fear is an excellent motivator?
    a. True
    b. False

3. According to Ms. Juarez-Lim, *presences* means:
    a. Being stylish and trendy in your dress in order to leave a lasting impression
    b. An ability to bring together all of the people and mentors who have helped shape who you are and do project those images or attitudes as your own
    c. An ability to present oneself in a way that conveys credibility and to influence others through your leadership and communication skills
    d. Physically being present in the building, meeting, workplace, and so on

CHAPTER 9

Civility in Action: Applications

Don't discount the power of your words. The thought that they might cause unnecessary hurt or discomfort should inform every conversation.

—P.M. Forni

One common and relatively easy-to-implement civility solution is to teach civil communication as a *civility in action* initiative. Communication is an essential skill for leaders in any sector. But, for supervisors who are responsible for managing teams, such as in hospitality, service industries, retail, or manufacturing, this skill becomes critical. And yet, many organizations do not spend sufficient time and resources ensuring that their leaders are effective communicators.

If we look at the manufacturing sector as an example, LMA Consulting Group, Claremont, California, has released the *Manufacturing and Distribution Skills Gap Report*, based on a skills gap survey conducted in conjunction with the APICS—Inland Empire chapter that focused on how manufacturers and distributors are adjusting to the new *business normal* in terms of their workforces.

The survey, which asked hiring managers and human resources professionals about recruiting, training, and general employment trends in manufacturing and distribution, revealed that many of the soft skills needed to be a successful manufacturing employee were lacking in both existing workers and potential new hires. For current employers, 77.7 percent of the respondents stated that their own employees lack basic *presentation and communications skills* needed to be successful in their current positions, and that this lack of skill would impact future professional movement within the organization.

Closely following a gap in communication skills is the *inability to problem solve* or come up with ideas or alternatives to a situation or issue. In general, the manufacturing workforce is asking for direction from supervisors or managers, rather than initiating new ideas and solutions.

Core communication skill requirements of employers have not changed much over time. But, the emphasis on *collaborative work* has altered dramatically. A Harvard Business Review study[1] found that the time managers and employees spend on collaborative activities has increased by more than 50 percent in the past 20 years.

It is not a stretch to imagine that these gaps are likely common across sectors. Closer and comprehensive review of skills gaps across organizational—initially undertaken as a means of understanding why these workplaces were uncivil has informed the Civility Experts Inc. team that when general communication, problem-solving, and collaboration skills are lacking, one way to improve and encourage interactions at work is to make civility training generally, but social intelligence training specifically, a priority. This because social intelligence teaches people the following skills which can offset communication skills gaps, enable people who cannot problem solve on their own to ask questions, and builds trust such that people can collaborate more effectively.

Social intelligence training enables people to:

- Read verbal, nonverbal, contextual, and situational cues to interpret the mood, motivation, and needs of others
- Exhibit nonverbal, verbal, and situations cues appropriately
- Be present, for example, pay attention to what is going on around them
- Recognize when gestures, language, behavior, or approach is grounded in culture, generation, or gender nuances
- Pick up on very subtle changes in tone and behavior, for example, to sense when a mood shifts
- Learn unwritten rules, for example, unspoken and unwritten expectations for how to live in a certain environment, for example, aspects of workplace culture

---

[1] Cross, R., R. Rebele, and A. Grant. 2016. "Collaborative Overload." *Harvard Business Review,* December 20, 2016, https://hbr.org/2016/01/collaborative-overload

- Learn written and known rules, for example, codes of conduct, regulation
- Become self-aware, for example, of one's own social style
- Adapt one's social style to what is appropriate or required for a certain situation
- Adapt to change quickly, for example, because of the ability to shift social gears when necessary
- Respond to events calmly, for example, because of the ability to anticipate and/or monitor
- Recognize appropriate time to ask questions
- See aspects of personality that are otherwise unnoticed
- Send positive first impression
- Make others feel at ease
- Build trust, for example, because of paying attention
- Be a better listener
- Be cordial, for example, approachable
- Show humility, for example, recognize when help is needed
- Read emotions, for example, be empathetic when needed

When leaders have high social intelligence combined with some experience interacting with others in the workplace context, for example, they know the general expectations for the workplace culture, they know the industry jargon, have some knowledge of the terms and processes, they can apply their social intelligence in a way that fosters social acuity.

Indicators of Social Acuity

Leaders need to have high *social acuity*, that is, they need to have a keen social sense. They must be consistently accurate and timely in their perceptions and assessments of social settings. They need to know how to:

- Read contextual cues
- Be attentive to the nuances of workplace culture
- Navigate politics in union environments
- Identify who will be an ally and who will be a challenge
- Build trust
- Repair when a trust is broken

- Consider contextual aspects when timing everything from greetings, to feedback to workplace coaching and performance reviews
- Communicate in a way that leaves everyone involved in the interaction feeling valued
- Acknowledge differences that make a difference, for example, related to gender, culture, generation
- Give timely and effective feedback
- Monitor and manage nonverbal cues to boost credibility and perceived competence
- Adapt supervisory approach and style to meet the needs of individual workers
- Apply adult learning principles
- Maintain credibility as a leader but still be perceived as approachable by the production team

Clearly, it takes time to build communication skills, and when contexts and teams are continually changing, a person must apply continuous learning in order to keep up with expectations and to be effective in various settings. Building on 20+ years in manufacturing, Christian Masotti, in collaboration with Civility Experts Inc. has compiled a Social Competence Toolkit for Supervisors that includes 10 communication strategies with ready-to-use checklists. While Mr. Masotti's application was in manufacturing, the strategies are very effective in other sectors too. Review and application of these tools can expedite a supervisor's ability to acquire critical communication skills.

Masotti & Bayer Commonsense Social Competence Strategy #1: Wait for It

This strategy is about pausing—being deliberate about being present, listening, and suspending judgment.

- Pause deliberately to assess the situation.
- Resist saying anything immediately.
- Suspend your thoughts, for example, do not make assumptions, do not jump to conclusions, set aside any bias or expectations.

- Listen to the other person.
- Pay attention to the context, for example, what is going on around you.
- Watch the other person's nonverbal cues.
- Ask questions using a calm, polite tone.
- Avoid starting your sentences with "I" in an effort to be other-focused.
- Be self-aware. Pay attention to when you make snap judgments and work to understand why you have jumped to conclusions and then set those judgments aside.

Masotti & Bayer Commonsense Social Competence Strategy #2: Just Be Nice

This strategy is about extending common courtesies and choosing to be humankind.

- Pause, wait… take a breath, compose yourself, think about what you will say or do *before* you do it.
- Assume the best of others; try to set aside any personal issues, history with the individual, personal needs, known biases, and so on.
- Consider social protocol. What do the social rules (written or unwritten) suggest is the appropriate response or behavior in this setting and/or situation?
- Think about what you want to happen next, for example, how do you want to be perceived, how do you want the other person to feel, what do you want the outcome of the interaction or communication to be?
- Consider the time and place, for example, is this the right time for the communication? Should you go somewhere private? Do you need a third party to witness? Does the other party need time to compose himself or herself?
- Be kind:
  - Choose words and/or actions that show you at your best and do not cause harm to the other person.
  - Make eye contact as a way of acknowledging others.

- ° Extend general greetings, for example, say hello.
- ° Maintain a calm and moderate tone, for example, do not yell.
- ° Avoid swearing.
- Close with a verbal or physical handshake, for example, shake hands, say thank you for X, look the person in the eye. *Or*, acknowledge and close the interaction verbally, for example, say, "So, we are all good then?" or "See you tomorrow then" or something to show you anticipate a positive and future interaction.

Masotti & Bayer Commonsense Social Competence Strategy #3: Get Out There and Talk to People

This strategy is about being intentional in how you engage with others socially:

- Always keep your head up when passing others or walking through a workspace, halls, parking lot, and so on.
- Even if you do not know people, make it your habit to glance at them. Practice noticing things about people; what they are wearing, expressions, and so on.
- Practice keeping an approachable, friendly look on your face.
- Be deliberate about exhibiting open postures: do not sit with your arms crossed, take your hands out of your pockets, remove sunglasses when talking to people indoors, extend an open palm for a handshake.
- When you know people (even if you do not know their names), make eye contact and smile.
- If you cannot stop to talk, wave or nod hello, but do not ask a question such as, "How are you?" while you continue walking or moving.
- If you have time to stop and chat. Stop. Turn your shoulders square with the other person, greet him or her, move to within 24 inches of the other person, and engage. Set aside all other distractions while you do so.

- If you have to break eye contact or move your attention to someone or something else for a minute, for example, check your watch, or acknowledge another person, say, "excuse me" before you do it, or say, "sorry about that" after you do it.
- As you are chatting, make a point to focus on the other person. Ask him or her questions and wait for the answers. Try to avoid talking about yourself.
- If you did not shake hands when you greeted the person, and when context and culture suggest its appropriate, extend an exit handshake.
- If you are legitimately busy, do not stop and pretend to pay attention. Simply state that you are glad to see the person, but are unable to visit at this time, and then wish the person a happy day and move on.

Masotti & Bayer Commonsense Social Competence Strategy #4: Apply Continuous Learning to Connect With People

This strategy is about recognizing that every interaction is a learning opportunity.

- Treat people with respect from the beginning so that when you need to approach them for help, they see you as someone they can trust who values them.
- Assume that someone, at some time, somewhere has experienced this same situation.
- Assume that you are not the only person to have an idea.
- Always ask the people doing the job, ask them directly, face-to-face.
- Approach people at the appropriate time.
- Be respectful in your tone, do not assume people have an obligation to help you just because you are a supervisor.
- Ask targeted questions, for example, not open ended.
- Admit you need help.

- Listen for answer—do not interrupt, do not criticize or apply your personal biases, opinions, or beliefs.
- Do not dismiss anyone, you never know what information will be useful down the road, even if the information being shared at the time is not relevant, use the interaction as an opportunity to build rapport and trust.
- Consider that one person may not have all the answers, but the collective probably does.
- Acknowledge the sharing and the information, let the person sharing with you know you appreciate their help.
- Give credit when you use the information down the road.
- Share the information with others, for example, do not hoard it now that you have it.
- Avoid going back to the same person more than once; this can cause strain within the team. Instead build a relationship with each member of the team, this builds credibility.

Masotti & Bayer Commonsense Social Competence Strategy #5: Always Tell the Truth

This strategy is about relational wealth. If you want to build trust, here are some communication habits you should adopt:

- Make a point to be honest with everyone, not just some people.
- Be consistent, for example, always tell the truth; do not pick and choose when to be honest.
- Be honest when delivering both good and bad news.
- Be direct, tell the whole truth versus a piece or version of the truth, for example, instead of saying you are being fired for lateness, an indirect version, is saying, "You know, lateness is one of the metrics we watch."
- Assume the best of people, but do not immediately trust everything people say; ask strategic questions.
- Look people in the eye when you are communicating the truth.

- Be deliberate in your communication—choose your words carefully and say exactly what you mean, do not sugarcoat or be vague.
- Avoid pretending you have authority or power you do not have—be honest about your abilities and influence.
- Do your due diligence before making promises—ensure you can follow through before you say what you can and will do.
- Pick an appropriate time to be truthful.
- Consider privacy and confidentiality.
- Monitor your tone, for example, do not be harsh.
- Avoid apologizing for telling the truth, for example, "I'm sorry to have to tell you X, but…."
- Give people a minute to absorb what you are telling them.
- Keep being truthful, even when others are dishonest, and/ or even when no one seems to notice. People do notice, and there is often documentation to support your efforts.

Masotti & Bayer Commonsense Social Competence Strategy #6: Ask Strategic Questions

This strategy is about acknowledging that you cannot know everything—you must be able to ask for help:

- See people as resources. Assume you can learn from them.
- Be clear in your own mind about what exactly you need to know—what information are you seeking?
- Watch for the appropriate time to approach someone to ask questions, for example, do not bother employees right before lunch or during lunch or breaks. This is their personal time, and they may resent your intrusion. Consider approaching at the end of the shift or just after a break or lunch.
- Consider privacy and confidentiality.
- Do not interrupt when the other person is talking.
- Do not assume you already know the answer to the question you are asking.
- Do not assume that the answer is correct or factual, be sure.

- Do not assume that only one person has the answer or information you seek. Ask more than one person if possible.
- Do not assume that one person speaks for the whole group.
- Monitor your postures and nonverbal communication when listening, for example, avoid condescending or impatient gestures.
- Listen with *TING*.
- Ask a specific question, start with one question only. Avoid bombarding the person with many questions at once.
- Chose a specific question for a specific purpose, for example:
  - Ask a how is your day question to gage morale or attitude.
  - Ask a get to the point question to hold someone accountable for a misbehavior.
  - Ask a what would happen if question to get someone to share information or help resolve a problem.
- Do not expect a thank you and do not say things like, "You owe me one," extend the gesture with no expectation of reciprocity.

Masotti & Bayer Social Competence Strategy #7: Build Resilience (Learn to Take a Punch)

This strategy is about being of strong will, staying positive, and not taking things too personally:

- Show people how the work they do is valued on the job, for example, why is enduring the hardship worth it?
- Make people aware of the type of challenges they may face on the job.
- Provide opportunities for people to see how others managed those challenges in the past.
- Build your own resilience, for example, model resilient behavior, for example:
  - Have a positive attitude.
  - Name your fears, and face them.
  - Set small achievable personal goals ongoing so that you can experience success.

- ° Encourage others, for example, foster optimism.
- ° Do not take yourself too seriously, for example, have a sense of humor.
- ° Take advantage of social supports around you, for example, ask for help when you need it.
- Encourage autonomy.
- Provide opportunities to practice coping strategies.
- Build *timeout* opportunities into daily routine, for example, make sure people get breaks.
- Incorporate positive language, for example, affirmations, into workplace slogans and mottos.
- Provide team supports, for example, buddy and mentor programs.

Masotti & Bayer Commonsense Social Competence Strategy #8: Foster Collaboration

This strategy is about how to build engagement and rapport:

- Be approachable.
- Do not take yourself too seriously.
- Be able to say "I don't know."
- Be transparent.
- Assume there are people in the room smarter than you are.
- Acknowledge the experience, skills, and credentials of others.
- Be curious, ask questions.
- Ask for help.
- Take notes, show that you are serious about the information you are seeking.
- Review the process that support collaboration.
- Offer support, with no strings attached.
- Be honest about what you know.
- Share what you know.
- Stick to the facts when you can, avoid opinion.
- Thank others who share with you.
- Credit others with information they share with you that you pass on.

- Strive to exceed expectations, for example, give more than is required.
- Implement process to ensure that all collaborators have an opportunity to share.
- Set ground rules for communication in collaboration settings.
- Invite varied opinions and discussion—disagreement is sometimes a good thing.
- Encourage wild ideas, creativity, and innovation.
- Create a psychologically safe environment where others feel free to speak.
- Maintain confidentiality, where applicable.

Masotti & Bayer Commonsense Social Competence Strategy #9: Be Hardy

This strategy is about recognizing your physical and mental limitations and planning for them:

- Anticipate and plan for a physically demanding environment, for example, consider what you and/or your team need to work well related to:
  - Noise.
  - Deadlines.
  - Moving equipment.
  - Moving vehicles.
  - Ventilation: Quality and noise associated with.
  - Repetitive motion.
  - Safety equipment, for example, that hinders movement.
  - Physical barriers to communication.
  - Tight spaces.
  - Large, open spaces.
  - Difficulty related to equipment.
  - Range of motion required.
  - Time standing.
  - Distance to areas you need to go to on the job, for example, parking to work site.
  - Availability of washrooms.

- Allowable breaks.
- Allergens.
- Chemicals.
- General morale.
- Temperature in the room.
- Availability of food and water.
- Availability of first aid or emergency equipment.
- Take care of your personal needs:
  - Sleep when you can and for a reasonable amount of time.
  - Keep up with regular body maintenance: dentist, eye doctor, doctor.
  - Have supply of any required medications on hand.
  - Exercise regularly.
  - Eat a healthy diet.
  - Practice effective stress management.
  - Practice good hygiene, for example, hair, nails, shaving.
  - Make it a habit to keep clothes clean and in good repair.
  - Maintain safety standards, for example, wear safety equipment.
- Watch for typical *look and behavior* when you or others are doing the job. If there is variance, or off-standard look and behavior, consider if that behavior is impacting performance. If it is, you need to address what you are seeing.
  - You do not need to know the reason, you just identify and call out the behavior, for example, to prevent an injury.
  - Ask questions to discover cause of off-standard behavior, for example, due to:
    1. Drugs.
    2. Alcohol.
    3. Nervous breakdown.
    4. High stress.
    5. External situation, for example, personal trauma.
    6. Illness.
    7. Depression.
    8. Hunger.
    9. Exhaustion.
    10. Distress.

Masotti & Bayer Commonsense Social Competence Strategy #10: Be Responsible

This strategy is about being an adult at work—recognizing you are accountable and approaching your work with maturity:

- Run your own race: Decide what you want out of life and make a plan to achieve it.
- Establish personal standards, for example :
  - Morning routing.
  - Daily exercise.
  - Eat healthy.
  - Only take jobs that pay minimum of X.
  - Do not engage in, or endorse, illegal activity.
  - Pay what I owe.
- Establish personal policies, for example:
  - Do not lie.
  - Always do more than is expected.
  - Always consider how my actions will impact others.
  - Never steal.
  - Always save someone else some hardship or misery if I can.
  - Give without expecting anything in return.
- Clarify expectations of others.
- Make promises, but only if you can keep them.
- Learn to say no.
- Learn to apologize.
- Accept compliments.
- Accept apologies from others.
- Invite feedback.
- Learn from mistakes.
- Forgive yourself for mistakes.
- Accept that you cannot fix, help, or save everyone; people have to learn to take responsibility for themselves.
- Be sure you know what your specific responsibilities are, for example, job tasks.
- Take ownership of our own learning.

Recommended Homework

For homework for this chapter, please take the time to review the preceding checklists and self-assessments. Take the time to reflect on these two areas with honesty and sincerity and really look at areas where you are finding success and areas that are currently lacking and in need of further development. Keep in mind that the only true way to make a change and see improvement is to be honest with yourself and be open and willing to make changes.

Once you have taken the time to review and assess, complete the following personal development chart.

Area of Civil Communication to Improve	Step to Take to Improve

Figure 9.1

Test Yourself

1. It is important for leaders to have high social acuity because:
   a. They must be attentive to the nuances of workplace culture.
   b. They must build and repair trust in the workplace.
   c. They must communicate in a way that leaves everyone involved in the interaction feeling valued.
   d. All of the above.
   e. None of the above.
2. True or false, waiting is a key element of effective and powerful communication?
   a. True.
   b. False.
3. Which is not a Masotti commonsense social competence strategy.
   a. Be hardy.
   b. Gain power.
   c. Foster collaboration.
   d. Ask strategic questions.

CHAPTER 10

Assignments

Assignment #1

Personal Values Review

Checklist for Personal Values

Adapted from C. Roberts, Fifth Discipline Fieldbook. This exercise is designed to help you reach a better understanding of your most significant values.

Step 1: What I Value Most... From this list of values (both work and personal), select the 10 that are most important to you—as guides for how to behave, or as components of a valued way of life. Feel free to add any values of your own to this list. Then, narrow your list to just three values that you consider to be the most important to you. Think about why you choose these values and be able to describe what they mean to you to others:

Achievement	Friendships	Physical challenge
Civility	Growth	Pleasure
Adventure	Having a family	Power and authority
Affection (love and caring)	Helping other people	Privacy
Arts	Helping society	Public service
Challenging problems	Honesty	Purity
Change and variety	Independence	Quality of what I take part in
Close relationships	Influencing others	Quality relationships
Community	Inner harmony	Recognition (respect from others, status)
Competence	Integrity	Religion
Competition	Intellectual status	Reputation

Cooperation	Involvement	Responsibility and accountability
Country	Job tranquility	Security
Creativity	Knowledge	Self-respect
Decisiveness	Leadership	Serenity
Democracy	Location	Sophistication
Ecological awareness	Loyalty	Stability
Economic security	Market position	Status
Effectiveness	Meaningful work	Supervising others
Efficiency	Merit	Time freedom
Ethical practice	Money	Truth
Excellence	Nature	Wealth
Excitement		
Fame	Order (tranquility, stability, conformity)	Work under pressure
Fast living	Personal development	Work with others
Financial gain	Freedom	Working Civility

Assignment #2

Consider how different contexts related to long-term incivility can impact us, for example:

- What happens when you are surrounded by people who have experienced incivility, such as genocide, concentration camps, or persecution?
- World events, for example, acts of terrorism
- Policies, for example, equal rights
- Political events, for example, dictatorships
- Natural events, for example, catastrophes from which whole communities never completely recover
- Trends and social influences, for example, social media
- Culture, for example, you live in a place where incivility such as war is a constant

Choose 3 of the preceding examples of various contexts and write a 1,500-word essay expressing and rationalizing your viewpoint.

Assignment #3

Listed next are several training case scenarios[1]. Choose one of the examples and carefully review the information provided. Then, answer the following questions:

1. What workplace conditions, policies, or issues may have contributed to the problem? Be as specific as you can.
2. What types of training (aside from civility) would traditionally be offered to address the problem that was identified?
3. If you were the consultant called in to help with this problem, describe in detail the questions you would ask, and the approach you would take to assessing the problem and the skills that need to be trained.
4. Are there any potential barriers or considerations you would address to ensure success of the training?
5. Based on what you know about civility, what specific aspects of civility would you aim to improve with your training solution?

Scenarios:

1. An *aerospace company* had identified that their employee engagement (EE) program was not resulting in the innovation and efficiency improvements they had anticipated. Assessment interviews with employee involvement team leads had indicated the following:
   a. Low attendance at team meetings—although the meetings were *mandatory*
   b. Poor engagement by those who attended meetings
   c. Low percentage of projects initiated by the teams were completed
   d. Poor scores on mandatory team building skills training
2. A *gypsum manufacturing company* contacted a training service provider when they were struggling to keep team morale high. They had identified interpersonal issues between two groups of employees: the long-term experienced *veterans* and the newer, younger, college

---

[1] Adapted from fieldwork in partnership with Workplace Education Manitoba.

graduate employees—two of whom were new managers. Uncivil behaviors such as sabotage, fist-fights, inappropriate languages, and refusal to work shifts together were common.

3. A *metal duct work manufacturing* company of 16,000 contacted the training solutions provider, asking for *diversity and cultural training* for its supervisors and team leads. The company had determined that error rates and waste had continually increased over 36 months, and they attributed this to communication barriers between the large Filipino production team and the supervisors.

4. A *pharmaceutical dispensing or packaging company* was concerned about how the night shift was falling short, by about 30 percent, of meeting its production goals. The day shift was having no issue. The production gap was causing a rift between day- and night-shift employees as well as shift leads and managers.

5. Based on rapid growth in the industry, *a printing company* anticipated having to manage significant change in the workplace related to employee recruitment, retention, job task assignments, and general shifts to workloads as well as to how the individuals and teams work together. The organization knew it needed to build adaptive capacity but did not know where to start.

Assignment #4

End in Mind—Step 1 in the Three-Step Process for Devising a Civility Initiative

Questions to Ask

1. What exactly do you want to happen as a result of the initiative? Stated differently, what is the purpose of building a culture of civility? *Note*: Using the Civility Experts *Symptoms of Viral Incivility* checklist can help you identify what you do not want. And/or, review of the list of 32 possible positive outcomes of civility training included at the beginning of Chapter 2 in the Civility at Work: A Civility Initiative Toolkit can help you identify what you do want.

2. Why do you want whatever it is that you want?

3. What specifically is the benefit or impact to the employee(s), and/or to the organization, if you get what you want?

4. Are there any drawbacks or unfavorable consequences to you, the team, or the organization if you get what you want?

5. What evidence do you have that the outcome you want could, or would, in fact result from the initiative? And, are you prepared if the outcomes are different than you expected?

6. Are your goals realistic, for example, SMARTER; specific, measurable, attainable, realistic, time-set and/or timely, evaluated, and rewarding or rewarded?

Practice writing a SMARTER goal here:

Assignment #5

Adapted From the Work of Stephen Carter:
Assumptions About Civility.

This exercise measures your understanding about and your commitment to the concepts surrounding civility. Consider engaging with others who are studying civility to compare notes and opinions on this topic.

This is for an open discussion for the entire group.

1. Our duty to be civil toward others does not depend on whether we like them or not.

2. Civility creates not merely a negative duty not to do harm, but an affirmative duty to do good.

3. We must come to the presence of our fellow human beings with senses of awe and gratitude.

4. Civility assumes that we will disagree; it requires us not to mask our differences but to resolve them respectfully.

5. Civility requires that we listen to others with the knowledge of the possibility that they are right and we are wrong.

6. Civility requires that we express ourselves in ways that demonstrate our respect for others.

7. Civility allows criticism of others, and sometimes even requires it.

Assignment #6

Review the following notes and write a 1,000 to 1,500-word essay summarizing why you think work is so stressful and causing depression.

According to the Human Solutions Report, *Under Pressure*, respondents indicated that on average, job stress accounted for 73 percent of their overall life stress. Further, 59 percent of the respondents said that the quality of their home and family life was sometimes impacted by job stress and 16 percent said that job stress frequently impacted their personal and family life.

With a whopping 96 percent of employees polled in a workplace study conducted by Pearson and Porath, experiencing rudeness at work, and knowing that the majority of people say stress at work is the largest contributor to their overall stress, it is not unreasonable to infer that rudeness is contributing to the stress. And, it is easy to see that work simply is not much fun for a lot of people.

To solve the incivility problem in our workplaces, we need to change how we work. We need to create workplaces that support a culture of learning where thinking is best practice. We need to build a capacity for civil behavior by giving people the skills they need to make better decisions and to contribute to reducing the stress and incivility in our workplaces. We need to imbed civility in our workplace policies and procedures, into our organizational values and mission statements, into our job descriptions and codes of conduct, and into our hiring and evaluation practices. Civility has to become a core element in the character of our organizations. Stated directly, civility in the workplace is a change imperative for organizations expecting to survive, and thrive, in the new world of work.

Lew Bayer, President, Civility Experts Worldwide

- In many workplaces, the pull toward incivility gets stronger because:
  - Choosing incivility is easier than choosing civility

- There are more rewards than consequences for being uncivil
- We are not learning to be civil through our experiences and interactions at work, and without experiencing civility, it is difficult to understand the benefits of it
- The written and unwritten rules have changed so much and are changing ongoing, and so many of us just are not sure of the current expectations and so, we mirror the behavior of whomever seems to be leading at a specific time, in a specific context
- Civility in the workplace has been dismissed for a very long time as something *nice to have* and so civility is rarely strategically or formally taught
- Even when they know what civility is, many people simply do not have the skills they need to exhibit civility in an ever-changing workplace
- In a workplace context, where incivility can be attributed to a lack of experiential education, the plan for fostering a culture civility in the workplace is to change their experience. We do this by:
  - Creating an environment where positive change (learning) is required and supported—this is to replace an environment where bad habits and negativity have been endorsed over positive change or learning
  - Encouraging (and in fact requiring by way of policy and procedure) this positive change in the form of behavior in four key skill areas that underpin the ability to be civil
- The Civility Culture Compass® offers a model for a creating a culture of civility in your workplace. The compass outlines a proactive, competency-based approach to shifting organizational culture from toxic and negative to respectful and positive. The Civility Culture Compass® is used to assess four organizational conditions, which when *ideal*, as described next, increase the success of civility initiatives. These conditions are:
  - Change
  - Alignment

- ○ Engagement
- ○ Readiness
- Civility as a core competency requires that an individual can exhibit certain measurable, and related knowledge, skills, abilities and commitments, and to do so consistently, in a way, and at a standard prescribed for application in a specific context, for example, a workplace, in a way that is deemed effective for that context.
- A needs assessment is a systematic exploration of the way things are and the way they should be. These *things* are usually associated with organizational and/or individual performance[2].
- The purpose of conducting a needs assessment is to better understand the reason why things are the way they are, rather than the way they should be and how we want them to be. Analyzing the issues and factors that are creating the current situation helps us know what the solution is to get us where we want to be, and where, when, and how we will apply that solution.
- One of the key reasons a needs assessment is completed prior to launching a training plan is to manage resources.
- There are two typical approaches to completing a workplace civility assessment:
  - ○ Help people identify performance issues and consider what skills gaps are causing the issues as well as how planned training can help to solve them.
  - ○ Taking a big picture view of the whole organization. Consider current, present, and future activities and goals, and then develop training plans to meet the identified current and anticipated training needs.
- The recommended assessment process is:
  - ○ Phase 1: Complete a general organizational culture assessment.

---

[2] Rouda, R.H.,m and M.E. Kusy. 1995. "Needs Assessment: The First Step." *Needs Assessment the First Step,* http://flash.lakeheadu.ca/~mstones/needs_assessment.html

○ Phase 2: If general organizational culture assessment identifies issues related to incivility, administer assessments to identify which one or more of the four civility culture conditions: readiness, change, alignment, and engagement, is not ideal.

○ Phase 3: When one or more of the four civility culture conditions has been identified as not ideal, conduct further targeted assessments in that specific foundational area.

- One of the ways the compass can save organizations time and money is because sometimes, once the influencing conditions are restored to *ideal*, the incivility symptom is resolved and no training is necessary.

- If civility is a problem in your workplace, talking about it is not likely going to resolve your issues. Discourse certainly has its place, but when habits are ingrained, expectations not clearly defined, and/or when people do not know what they do not know, training is how to solve the problem.

- The Civility Culture Compass® outlines four conditions, which when met, increase the likelihood that efforts to build a culture of civility will be successful. The compass also depicts four key skills that collectively make up the overall competency in civility. These are the skill areas in which training is planned and implemented.

- The Civility Competency Matrix® is a training tool that details the knowledge, skills, and abilities for each of the four key skill areas that build competency in civility. These skill areas are:

○ Continuous learning—Learning strategies for learning ongoing

○ Social intelligence—The ability to effectively identify and interpret nonverbal, verbal, and contextual cues; to adapt social style; and to apply written and unwritten social rules—this enables you to get along with others

○ Systems thinking—The ability to see the big picture, to distinguish patterns, to recognize interconnectedness of the systems, and to see your role within the systems

- ○ Cultural competence—Being able to appreciate fundamental cultural differences and values that impact workplace relationships and doing so in a way that benefits the parties involved and leverages differences—real or imagined
- Training in one or more of these four key skills areas under *ideal* conditions can result in measurable impact to the bottom line.

In *Manufacturing Civility,* (Propriety Publishing with Social Motion Publishing, 2020), which I had the pleasure of contributing to, Christian Masotti, the leading expert on civility as a continuous improvement strategy, suggests that,

> …in manufacturing environments, true workplace culture, i.e., not what leadership presumes it to be, or describes it as, is reflected in the day to day experience of the organizations' employees. Day-to-day experience impacts performance and the achievement of overall key performance indicators, including safety and quality, is a direct reflection of engagement. If you want to improve engagement, you need to create a culture where the daily experience includes civility.

Mr. Masotti is not alone in his thinking. He expresses a notion that we at Civility Experts Inc. have long endorsed, and I suggest that the idea applies to all sectors, not just manufacturing. The research agrees. In a study of companies with over 500 employees, researchers found that 71 percent of the managers felt that employee engagement was one of the most important factors in overall company success[3].

However, despite employee engagement being viewed as a positive companywide, the majority of employees are disengaged at work. According to Gallup data, only 33 percent of employees reported they are engaged at work. Low engagement can be caused by several factors, including lack of recognition by managers, poor company communication, and not

---

[3] "Why Is Employee Engagement Important to Company Success?" *Social-Chorus*, August 10, 2020, https://socialchorus.com/blog/employee-experience/employee-engagement-key-to-company-success/

being aligned with the mission of the company. It is clear that company leaders need to start viewing employee engagement as a strategic business objective because engaged employees lead to long-term employee retention, higher levels of productivity, and improved quality of work.

Talent Culture World of Work reports that:

- Increasing employee engagement investments by 10 percent can increase profits by 2,400 U.S. dollars per employee, per year. (Source: Workplace Research Foundation).
- Highly engaged employees are 38 percent more likely to have above-average productivity (source: Workplace Research Foundation).
- Companies that foster engaged brand ambassadors in their workforce report an average of 2.69 sick days taken annually per employee, compared to companies with weak engagement efforts, reporting an average of 6.19 sick days (source: Workplace Research Foundation).
- Companies with engaged employees, outperform those without by 202 percent (source: Dale Carnegie).
- Companies who implement regular employee feedback have turnover rates that are 14.9 percent lower than for employees who receive no feedback (source: Gallup).
- Only about 25 percent of the business leaders have an employee engagement strategy (source: Dale Carnegie).

Building on the preceding Workplace Research Foundations findings, I would argue that hands down, civility training is one of the most time- and cost-effective ways to invest in employee engagement. Many forward-thinking organizations are latching onto the idea of civility training. This is due in part to the solid business case, for example, as highlighted in *The 30% Solution: How Civility Increases Engagement, Retention and Profitability* (Bayer, Motivational Press 2016) The benefits of incorporating civility into the workplace, as detailed in research by Weber and Shadwick, include up to 30 percent more revenue than competitors and four times increased likelihood that employees will be highly engaged. Further, civility training could result in your organization being 20 percent more likely to report reduced turnover—all of these outcomes are both measurable and significant.

In addition, employers are beginning to see the link between workplace wellness and stress at work. Increasingly we are understanding that incivility is the root cause of much of this stress. When organizations are confronted with alarming statistics like the U.S. Center for Disease Control stating that by 2020 (yes, currently), depression will rank second to ischemic heart disease as the leading cause of workplace illness.

Some of the Causes of Workplace Depression

In case you did not know:

- Research by Morneau Shepell and the Mental Health Commission of Canada found that Canadian employees report *workplace stress as the primary cause of their mental health problems or illness, with depression and anxiety noted as the top two issues.*
- According to the Human Solutions Report, respondents indicated that *job stress accounted for 73 percent of overall life stress.*
- OpenSourceWorkplace.com suggests that *low morale among employees, stress, and a hostile workplace among others are major causes for uncivil behaviors in the work environment.* When employees are not happy or when they perceive their jobs are not being recognized and appreciated, they tend to exhibit stress and hostility.
- Mental health issues in the workplace are among the top concerns for organizations of all sizes. According to the Mental Health Commission of Canada (MHCC), *one in five Canadians experience a mental health problem or illness each year,* equating to approximately 500,000 employees unable to work every week due to mental health problems or illnesses.
- U.S. Center for Disease Control states that, effective in 2020, *depression is expected to be second only to heart disease as a source of the global burden of disease.* As chronic

disease and depressive disorders are increasingly recognized as major impediments to health, understanding the connection between them becomes of utmost importance to providing quality health care.

- A Forbes.com post, *Tackling Depression at Work as a Productivity Strategy*, shows that *depression is a leading cause of lost productivity* in the United States with an annual cost of 44 billion U.S. dollars to employers.

As you may have noted, the research paints a clear picture of the facts:

- Workplace incivility causes stress
- Stress contributes to depression
- Depression will be a debilitating issue that most organizations must manage moving into the next decade
- Leadership is to blame for the bulk of the incivility in the workplace

The bottom line is, how managers, supervisors, and leaders in general treat people at work matters. It matters a lot. In fact, according to Michelle McQuaid, a leading expert in Positive Psychology, 65 percent of the working adults said a better boss would make them happy. Only 35 percent said a raise would do the same[4].

---

[4] *Manufacturing Civility*, Introduction, Bayer and Masotti, Propriety Publishing with Social Motion Publishing, 2020.

CHAPTER 11

Answer Keys and Tools You Can Use

Answer Keys

Chapter 1

Test Yourself Answers

1. How many people die in genocides, which are global incivilities, every day?
   a. 10,000
   b. 5000
   c. *35,000*
   d. Over 100,000

2. When writing SMARTER goals for civility initiatives, the "E" refers to:
   a. Eliminate
   b. *Evaluate*
   c. Encourage
   d. Elaborate

3. Workplace "culture" is described by Masotti and Bayer as:
   a. How people dress and act at work
   b. The power division or hierarchy of a workplace
   c. *The day-to-day experience of living in a workplace*
   d. The tone of a company, for example, how people feel

Chapter 2

Test Yourself

1. Civility must be defined in a way that:
   a. *Makes people think differently*
   b. Distinguishes between civility and ethics
   c. Translates easily to other languages

2. According to Goleman, emotional intelligence includes how many aspects of intelligence:

a. Three

b. Six

c. *Two*

3. The three aspects of Civility Experts Inc. definition of civility are:

a. Character, confidence, attention

b. Effort, consistency, character

c. *Awareness, acknowledgment, effort*

Chapter 3

Test Yourself

1. According to research carried out by the Carnegie Institute of Technology, what percent of your financial success is due to skills in "human engineering"?

a. *85*

b. 45

c. 22

d. 91

2. Being able to bounce back after a disappointment or set back, big or small, and continue to move onward and upward is what Lei Han calls:

a. Tolerance

b. Stamina

c. *Resilience*

d. Optimism

3. *Soft skills* enable individuals to effectively apply technical skills and exhibiting soft skills requires some technical abilities; soft and technical skills are not necessarily useful independent of each other, this according to:

a. Barker and Knowles

b. *Lei Han*

c. Dr. Lewena Bayer

d. Steven Covey

Chapter 4

Test Yourself

1. What is the connection between change and civility?
   a. Implementing a civility initiative in your workplace will require change
   b. Change is a process and change initiative of civility is never truly finished
   c. The change initiative of civility in the workplace requires individuals to be *change-ready*
   d. *All of the above*
2. What is *not* a positive outcome of stress?
   a. Greater mental toughness
   b. Heighten awareness
   c. *Ability to multitask*
   d. Strengthened priorities
3. What is a trend that is effecting the way we work and do business?
   a. The weather
   b. Fashion trends
   c. *Demographic changes in the workforce*
   d. The cost of coffee

Chapter 5

Test Yourself

1. What are the four key civility skill areas?
   a. *Social intelligence, cultural competence, continuous learning, systems thinking*
   b. Social intelligence, cultural competence, continuous learning, respectful workplace policies
   c. Social intelligence, cultural competence, systems thinking, kindness
   d. Social intelligence, continuous learning, systems thinking, acknowledging mistakes
2. Which is *not* an element of the civility compass?
   a. Change
   b. *Acceptance*

    c. Alignment
    d. Readiness
3. How can we foster an environment of civility in a workplace?
    a. Creating an environment where positive change is required and
       supported
    b. Creating respectful workplace policies
    c. Encouraging (and requiring) positive behavior change in the four
       skills areas that underpin the ability to be civil
    d. *Both a and c*
    e. All of the above

Chapter 6

Test Yourself

1. What is not a part of SMARTER goal setting?
    a. Specific
    b. Measurable
    c. *Artistic*
    d. Teachable
2. What is step one of the assessment procedure?
    a. Complete a financial report to see if the company can afford this
       assessment
    b. *Complete a general organizational culture assessment*
    c. Complete an IQ assessment of all employees
    d. All of the above
3. How do employees express that they are in a high trust workplace?
    a. They feel empowered
    b. They have a shared sense of purpose
    c. They feel empowered to make decisions
    d. *All of the above*

Chapter 7

Test Yourself

1. Continuous learning involves the ability to....
    a. Set goals
    b. Self-reflect

    c. Gather insights

    d. *All of the above and more*

2. Systems thinking is...

    a. Computer operating systems that allow a business to function

    b. *The ability to see the bigger picture and view connections and patterns*

    c. Encouraging others

    d. Creating elaborate plans and proposals

3. In simplest terms, social intelligence is.....

    a. Knowing how to manipulate people

    b. Having a large social network

    c. Being outgoing and personable

    d. *The ability to get along with other people*

Chapter 8

Test Yourself

1. If you are unable to do every element on the checklist to building civility in your workplace, you should.....

    a. Avoid trying anything if you cannot do everything

    b. *Find the one element that will have the largest impact and start with that*

    c. Figure out what will be the cheapest aspect to bring into your workplace and start there

    d. None of the above

2. True or false, fear is an excellent motivator?

    a. True

    b. *False*

3. According to Ms. Juarez-Lim, *presences* means...

    a. Being stylish and trendy in your dress in order to leave a lasting impression

    b. An ability to bring together all of the people and mentors who have helped shape who you are and do project those images or attitudes as your own

    c. *An ability to present oneself in a way that conveys credibility and to influence others through your leadership and communication skills*

    d. Physically being present in the building, meeting, workplace, and so on.

Chapter 9

Test Yourself

1. It is important for leaders to have high social acuity because....
   a. They must be attentive to the nuances of workplace culture
   b. They must build and repair trust in the workplace
   c. They must communicate in a way that leaves everyone involved in the interaction feeling valued
   d. *All of the above*
   e. None of the above
2. True or false, waiting is a key element of effective and powerful communication?
   a. *True*
   b. False
3. Which is not a Masotti Commonsense Social Competence Strategy
   a. Be hardy
   b. *Gain power*
   c. Foster collaboration
   d. Ask strategic questions

ELEMENT	Average score 0 (–) and 10 (+)
Retention – general /overall	
Organizational capacity, e.g., maximizing resources	
Employee autonomy e.g., at production level	
Individual skills mastery and confidence	
Effective goal setting e.g., at production level	
Alignment of daily activity with organizational goals	
Accountability- generally	
Consistency in service delivery	
Respect in the workplace e.g., if respect = value, to what extent was each individual valued equally	
Exhibition of common courtesies	
Generalized reciprocity – that is, doing for others with no expectation of return, and doing things that are not required by the job description	

Figure 11.1

Civil discourse e.g., monitored tone, appropriate turn-taking, moderate volume, avoidance of harsh words or profanity	
Acceptance of diversity	
Team-orientation without being constantly directed to be a team	
Volunteer collaboration	
Innovation	
Thinking skills e.g., effective decision making, measured risk-taking	
Self-respect e.g., standing up for what one believes is right (courage on the job)	
Self-directed learning e.g., making independent choices to seek learning	
Culture of learning – encouraged by leaders and peers to pursue learning	
Change readiness – open to change and able to adapt in timely and effective way	
Engagement- defined as personal "buy-in" and trust of organization	
Understanding of shared purpose	
Overall trust	
Responsibility-taking without having to be directed e.g., claiming errors or apologizing	
Self-rated happy at work scores	
Hardiness e.g., physical bounce back- ability to withstand high physical stress	
Psychological safety e.g., extent to which employee would feel okay stating personal issue related to heath or otherwise	
Stress management e.g., did company offer supports?	
Restraint e.g., did people stop and think before taking action	
Overall morale	
Efficient (timely and concise) communication	

Figure 11.1 (Continued)

Tools You Can Use

The Workplace Civility Metrics Survey® by Masotti and Bayer, 2019

Symptoms of Viral Incivility© in the Workplace Assessment

Created by Lew Bayer, President Civility Experts Worldwide.

If world-scale incivilities—such as war and crime, political leaders' public temper tantrums, professional athletes' very unsportsmanlike conduct, over-the-top celebrity self-indulgence, rampant bigotry, and racism—do not have you convinced, consider how many of the following symptoms of viral incivility you have experienced in your own home, workplace, or community in the past two weeks:

- Persistent miscommunication, such as nonresponsiveness, misunderstandings, arguments, withholding of information, diminished morale and/or mood, negative attitudes, lack of energy, poor engagement, lowered confidence, and measurable lack of accountability
- Decreased productivity, increased lateness and laziness, reduced quality and quantity of output, diminished collaborative effort
- Increased customer service complaints, visible decrease in product and/or service standards
- Growing gap in alignment between personal or corporate goals and leadership's abilities, lack of integrity and ethics
- Inability to adapt effectively to change
- Inability to navigate cultural and communication barriers
- Increased difficulty recruiting and hiring competent personnel
- Difficulty identifying and practicing core values
- Lowered common sense, failure to attend to social cues and follow social conventions
- Increased disengagement; difficulty maintaining relationships; less involvement in social, civic, and community events

Covey—Speed of Trust Survey Tools

https://speedoftrust.com/speed-of-trust-measurement-tools

The Civility Culture Compass

https://civilityexperts.com/training-solutions/civility-workplace-assessments/

The Civility Culture Compass© devised by the team at Civility Experts Worldwide Inc. measures an organization relative to four conditions that need to be present and stable to ensure success of a civility initiative. These are:

- Change
- Engagement
- Readiness: logistical and skills-wise
- Alignment

Change—What is going on: past, present, and anticipated?

Engagement—How much do people choose to buy in (closely related to trust)?

Alignment—To what extent do the day-to-day activities align with the strategic goals?

Readiness—How prepared resources and skills-wise is the organization to implement change?

The outcomes also hint at which, if any, of the core competencies that underpin an ability to be civil, these are:

- Cultural competence
- Systems thinking
- Continuous learning
- Social intelligence

For more information and to use the free Civility Culture Compass tool, visit www.civilityexperts.com.

I Choose Civility: Steps to Adopting Civility as a Core Personal Value—Worksheet

I personally define civility as:

I can explain to others in my workplace that *civility* incorporates other personal values that they may have adopted in the following ways:

a. Civility includes honesty in that....

b. Civility includes accountability in that....

c. Civility includes integrity in that ....

d. Civility includes teamwork in that .....

e. Other: _____

f. I believe the outcomes or benefits of civility are:

g. To me:

h. To others:

i. To the workplace:

j. To the community:

I believe some behaviors that show I am civil include:

I believe that barriers to exhibiting civility include:

Perspectives on Change

I Believe that....	YES	Somewhat	NO
1. Change is inevitable			
2. Change is ongoing			
3. Change is mostly good			
4. Change is something I have no control over			
5. Change is something that happens to me			
6. Change is something I choose to actively participate in			
7. Change is always hard			
8. Change must be managed to be effective			
9. A person can never prepare enough for change			
10. Change always presents opportunities			

Figure 11.2

Culture Compass—Questionnaire

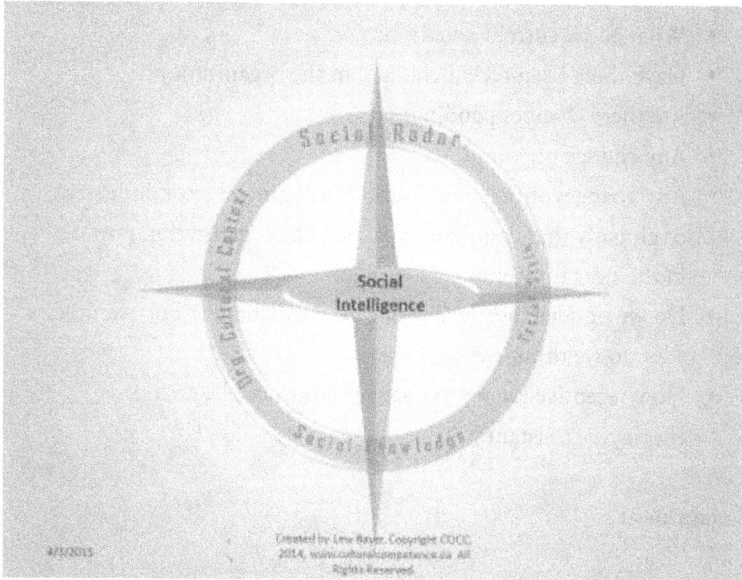

Figure 11.3

Civility Culture Compass—Four Conditions Assessment Questions

Alignment

- Do our organizational values include civility? If not, why not?
- To what extent are day-to-day activities, behaviors, policies, and processes currently aligned with the overriding goal, which, in the case of most civility initiatives, relates to building a better workplace?
- Is anything we are currently doing contrary to a culture of civility? (This is where we highly recommend even a short consult with a civility expert who may be able to pinpoint activities, policies, behaviors, and even processes that you do not immediately recognize as contributing to incivility in the workplace.)

Change

- What is the current situation?
- Have there been recent changes in the organization?
- Are there changes pending?
- Any change ongoing?
- Any changes anticipated in the community, sector, industry, or globally that could be impacting the organization now or in the near future?
- Do we understand the current need for change? For example, why do we think we need change?
- How receptive are we to change? For example, are our employees resistant?

Engagement

- To what extent do employees *choose* to participate in nonrequired workplace activities, for example, social events, work team sports, volunteer opportunities?
- Do employees trust us? And, do we trust them?
- Do employees show confidence in our decision making? Or, is there frequent push-back and resistance?
- Do employees seem happy at work?
- If we could not offer wage increases, how many employees would stay with us, for example, weather the storm and be loyal?
- When provided with opportunities for growth and training, do employees invest, for example, give of their own time or pay part of the cost?
- To what extent do employees support each other, for example, be accountable to each other, have each other's back, and/or engage personally/socially as well as at work?
- Overall, how would we rate collaboration in our workplace?
- Have we seen increases in sick days? Turnover? Grievances?
- How do our employees respond to change? For example, are they resilient? Adaptive? Resistant?

Readiness

Organizational

- Are we prepared to commit our time, money, and energy to this initiative?
- Do all stakeholders understand that this is an ongoing, and long-term investment?
- What specifically do we want to achieve?

Individual(s)

- Have we identified where our leaders and teams are *competency-wise* in the four key competency areas that support ability to be civil and build a culture of civility at work?
  - Social intelligence
  - Cultural competence
  - Continuous learning
  - Systems thinking
- Have we either trained someone in-house, or recruited or retained a qualified civility trainer to deliver the competency training we need to address the identified civility skills gaps?

Workplace Toxicity Exercise

Toxic behavior: Score *Nourishing* behavior:

Toxic behavior	Score	Nourishing behavior
Scowling, *stay-away* signals	_____	Keeping a positive, friendly expression
Throwing verbal barbs, *zingers*	_____	Kidding positively
Patronizing or *parenting* peopl	_____	Communicating *adult to adult*
Putting others down nonverbally	_____	Affirming others with positive *strokes*
Seeking approval excessively	_____	Speaking and acting assertively
Flattering others insincerely	_____	Giving honest compliments
Losing your temper frequently	_____	Pausing to listen and think

Playing *head games* with people	_____	Communicating openly and honestly
Disagreeing aggressively	_____	Dialoguing, exchanging views
Speaking dogmatically, inflexibly	_____	Expressing respect for others' ideas
Bragging, scoring *status points*	_____	Acknowledging the successes of others
Gossiping, violating confidences	_____	Keeping confidences
Breaking promises and agreements	_____	Making only promises you will keep
Joking at inappropriate times	_____	Using humor constructively
Monopolizing the conversation	_____	Sharing *air time* with others
Interrupting others frequently	_____	Hearing others out
Changing the subject capriciously	_____	Letting the topic *play out*
Complaining excessively	_____	Giving constructive suggestions
Giving someone the *hard sell*	_____	Suggesting, advising, negotiating
Insisting on getting one's way	_____	Compromising, helping others
Attacking or criticizing others	_____	Confronting constructively
Shooting down others' ideas	_____	Deferring judgment, listening, reflecting
Inducing guilt in others	_____	Persuading honestly; negotiating
Ridiculing other	_____	Supporting others; sympathizing
Giving unwanted advice	_____	Offering information, ideas, and options

Total Score: _____

So why *exactly* are our workplaces so stressful?

Good question. And, there is not an easy answer. I suspect the reasons vary depending on the workplace and on the people involved. We can blame change. For example, the following factors could have impact:

- Downsizing and restructuring
- Labor shortages
- Outsourcing
- Demographic shifts at work related to generations and cultures that make up the work team
- Economic insecurity

- Technology—and keeping up with the pace of change
- Trends in work style, for example, mobile executives, job-share programs

Overall, there seems to be much concern about job security. On average, Americans hold seven to eight different jobs before age 30. That makes it difficult to settle in and build rapport, never mind loyalty, if everyone is constantly got one foot out the door. And, difficult for employers to commit to training and long-term work contracts if they perceive a lack of loyalty or longevity in their work team.

Maybe it is a lack of leadership. After all, 25 percent of the managers who admitted to having behaved badly said they were uncivil because their leaders—their own role models—were rude. And, in a survey of 1,000 American executives, Michelle McQuaid, a leader in positive psychology interventions, found that only 35 percent of the Americans are happy at their jobs. And, 65 percent say a better boss would make them happy. And, only 35 percent say a pay raise will do the same thing.

Trust could be the reason. In *Edelman's Trust Barometer*, where results from 31,000 respondents representing 26 markets around the world were gathered, only 18 percent of those surveyed trust business leaders tell the truth. That is just slightly higher than the statistic for trusting government officials, which was only 13 percent.

Or, could it be our state of mind? Has all the stress and struggle to balance or get ahead left us physically less hardy and psychologically and emotionally less resilient? Job stress is increasingly recognized as a determinant of employee health and productivity. The experience of chronic stress is used in theoretical models as a predictor of increased risk of mental and physical problems, including chronic conditions such as heart disease, asthma, migraines, and ulcers.

Alarmingly, depression will rank second only to heart disease as the leading cause of disability worldwide by the year 2020, which can impact the workplace in areas such as bottom-line production and team work.

Leigh Steere is the cofounder of Managing People Better, LLC, a research organization that studies gender and generational differences in management styles and other management topics. She cited multiple causes of workplace depression.

"Work-related depression can have internal causes, external causes, or some of both," said Steere, offering these examples:

Internal Causes of Workplace Depression

- *A wrong-fit role.* A person feels called to be an artist but is working as an accountant.
- *Misalignment between company and personal values.* Keeping a job where there is ethical discomfort.
- *Working parent guilt.* "I like my work but feel I should be spending more time with my child."
- *Interpersonal discomfort.* Having to interface with people who are unpleasant or simply have different preferences, personalities, or work styles.
- *Work/life imbalance.* Workaholism and working long hours even when not asked and missing out on social connection outside of work, as well as hobbies, opportunities to relax, and exercise.
- *Introvert or extrovert stress.* A person may be an extrovert working in a role or environment where there is insufficient people interaction, or an introvert working in a bullpen-style office with constant interruptions, no privacy, and insufficient opportunity to *go internal.*
- *Financial struggles.* Maybe compensation and benefits do not meet the worker's basic needs.
- *Feeling trapped.* "I really want to leave this job, but I can't because (name your reason)." This may be a realistic assessment or a fear-based reaction.

External Causes of Workplace Depression

- *Unreasonable demands from management.* This may include requests to work frequent overtime, which interferes with home life.
- *Unclear guidance at work.* Some employees do not understand what is expected, so they feel they are in the dark and uncertain about whether they are doing a good job.

- *Poor project practices.* This may result in miscommunication, missed deadlines, blown budgets, or products that miss the mark. People want to be on a winning team that produces good work, but barriers to accomplishing this can contribute to depression.

- *Bullying at work.* Bullying behaviors faced in the workplace can be a huge problem for some employees, whether they are bullied by bosses, co-workers, or clients.

- *Low morale or low engagement at work. This may happen* due to the way a company spins information rather than being transparent, puts blame for leadership mistakes on others, nickel-and-dimes employees in the name of cost containment, and rewards ineffective managers.

- *Poor working conditions.* There are many conditions that become problematic when management will not take corrective action, for example, not letting employees take enough breaks or ignoring safety concerns and temperature discomfort[1].

---

[1] Laurie Sue Brockway et al., "Depression at Work: Is It You or the Job? - Depression Center - Everyday Health." *EverydayHealth.com,* https://everyday health.com/depression/depression-at-work-is-it-you-or-the-job.aspx

About the Author

You need only watch the evening news or pick up a newspaper to see that as humankind, we are in crisis. Whether it is leaders engaging in unsavory politics, war, and unrest, outcomes of a global health crisis, racism, workplace bullying, or children failing to exhibit common courtesies at school—incivility impacts all of us.

For more than 20 years, **Dr. Lewena Bayer**, CEO of Civility Experts Inc., 16-time published author and thought leader, has been striving to build better communities and workplaces all over the world. Lew, who believes that civility is its own reward, has been internationally recognized as a leading expert on civility in the workplace. With a focus on social intelligence and culturally competent communication, the team at Civility Experts Inc.—which includes 501 affiliates in 48 countries—has supported 1,000s of organizations in building better workplaces.

Index

OTHER TITLES IN THE HUMAN RESOURCE MANAGEMENT AND ORGANIZATIONAL BEHAVIOR COLLECTION

- *The Successful New CEO* by Christian Muntean
- *Breakthrough* by Saundra Stroope
- *Agility* by Michael Edmondson
- *Strengths Oriented Leadership* by Matt L. Beadle
- *Competencies at Work* by Enrique Washington and Bruce Griffiths
- *Manage Your Career* by Vijay Sathe
- *Leader Evolution* by Alan Patterson
- *Creating a Pathway to Your Dream Career* by Tom Kucharvy
- *Designing Creative High Power Teams and Organization* by Eric W. Stein
- *Fostering Creativity in Self and the Organization* by Eric W. Stein
- *You're A Genius* by Steven S. Taylor
- *Leading The Positive Organization* by Thomas N. Duening, Donald G. Gardner, Dustin Bluhm and Andrew J. Czaplewski
- *The Search For Best Practices* by Rob Reider
- *Effective Interviewing and Information Gathering* by Tom Diamante
- *Mastering Self-Motivation* by Michael Provitera

Concise and Applied Business Books

The Collection listed above is one of 30 business subject collections that Business Expert Press has grown to make BEP a premiere publisher of print and digital books. Our concise and applied books are for…

- Professionals and Practitioners
- Faculty who adopt our books for courses
- Librarians who know that BEP's Digital Libraries are a unique way to offer students ebooks to download, not restricted with any digital rights management
- Executive Training Course Leaders
- Business Seminar Organizers

Business Expert Press books are for anyone who needs to dig deeper on business ideas, goals, and solutions to everyday problems. Whether one print book, one ebook, or buying a digital library of 110 ebooks, we remain the affordable and smart way to be business smart. For more information, please visit www.businessexpertpress.com, or contact sales@businessexpertpress.com.

www.ingramcontent.com/pod-product-compliance
Lightning Source LLC
Chambersburg PA
CBHW061200220326
41599CB00025B/4546